TRADITION
AND VALOR

Robert V. Thomas

11/09/02

TRADITION AND VALOR

★ ★ ★

A Family Journey

by
Robert V. Morris

Sunflower University Press®

1531 Yuma • P. O. Box 1009 • Manhattan, Kansas 66505-1009 USA

Cover: J. B. Morris' Hampton Institute graduation portrait, 1912. Captain Brad Morris 1944-1945.

Layout by Lori L. Daniel

ISBN 0-89745-237-2

Sunflower University Press is a wholly-owned subsidiary of the non-profit 501(c)3 Journal of the West, Inc.

For My Father

Orators and ministers, educators and politicians, had extolled the Negro soldier as an example of courage and loyalty and skill to such a degree that the names of Old and New World military heroes of the colored races — Toussaint L'Ouverture, David Dumas, Chaka, Antonio Maceo, Peter Salem — were familiar enough to be used on any patriotic occasion.

— Ulysses Lee, *The Employment of Negro Troops*,
United States Army in World War II Special Studies, 4

— ★ ★ ★ —

. . . Is it not true that while we have fought our country's battles for one hundred fifty years, we have *not* gained our rights? No, we have gained them rapidly and effectively by our loyalty in time of trial.

Five thousand Negroes fought in the Revolution; the result was the emancipaton of slaves in the North and abolition of the African slave trade. At least three thousand Negro soldiers and sailors fought in the War of 1812; the result was the enfranchisement of the Negro in many Northern States and the beginning of a strong movement for general emancipation. Two hundred thousand Negroes enlisted in the Civil War, and the result was the emancipation of four million slaves, and the enfranchisement of the black man. Some ten thousand Negroes fought in the Spanish-American War, and in the twenty years ensuing since that war, despite many set backs, we have doubled or quadrupled our accumulated wealth.

— W. E. B. DuBois, "The Reward,"
The Crisis, XVI (September 1918), 217

MORRIS FAMILY

Lord Silas Crowe & Slave Woman
(1750) Virginia Plantation Owner

[1-2 Relatives Missing]

Joseph William & Salemma Morris
(1865-1955)
Leather Tanner — Shenandoah Valley,
Virginia & Covington, Georgia

Theapolis & Roberta Crowe
(1860?)
Madison County, Virginia

James Brad Morris, Sr.
(October 15, 1890 - December 1977)
Lawyer/Publisher — Atlanta, Georgia

Georgine Crowe
(1890 - December 1977)
Seamstress
Madison County, Virginia

James Brad Morris, Jr.
(February 19, 1919 - October 1, 1976)
Lawyer — Des Moines, Iowa

James Brad Morris III
(1948)
Lawyer

William Morris
(1957)
Lawyer

Robert Virgil Morris
(May 13, 1958)
Businessman/Author
Des Moines, Iowa

William II
(May 26, 1993)
Des Moines, Iowa

Jessica (May 12, 1987)
Robert (August 16, 1990)
Brandon (August 10, 1993)
Des Moines, Iowa

ROBERTS FAMILY

Robert E. Lee's Son (*Harry or Robert, Jr.?*) & Slave Sarah Lee
Virginia

Alexander Roberts & Ollie Jones — William Preston Bishop &
Mattie Bell Davis
Missouri

Alexander Whatt McCoy Roberts & Della Mae Bishop
Moline, Illinois

Arlene Janet Roberts, M.A.
Psychologist — Moline, Illinois

Contents

J. B. Morris, Sr. (right), Isaiah "Block" Blocker (center), and Jimmy Mitchell (standing), April 1968.

Foreword

*T*HEIR EYES SPARKLED as they told of their great adventures in a tone certain to capture the interest of the young men nearby. The racism they had conquered, the Germans they had killed, the French women they had romanced, and the blood they had spilled — all blended into a tale of *tradition* and *valor*.

It took my grandparents' 50th wedding anniversary in April of 1968 to bring these old men back together at the Savery Hotel in Des Moines, Iowa. J. B. Morris, Isaiah "Block" Blocker, and Jimmy Mitchell had survived and prospered through racial segregation, the First World War, and all that came after.

Even as a ten-year-old, the pride and pain of their story settled deep inside me, only to be unlocked three decades later. I pray my efforts will do these great men justice.

My father's long car rides to and from hunting and fishing destinations became on-going history sessions for my brother William and me.

Attorney J. B. Morris, Jr., took great pride in teaching us a variety of subjects, including his experience in World War II. His untimely death at age 57 still pains me, but I take comfort in knowing that his story lives and speaks through me, and now this book.

R. V. M.

Part One
J. B.

★ ★ ★

To describe my mother would be to write about a hurricane in its perfect power. Or the climbing, falling colors of a rainbow. . . .

Maya Angelou, *I Know Why the Caged Bird Sings*

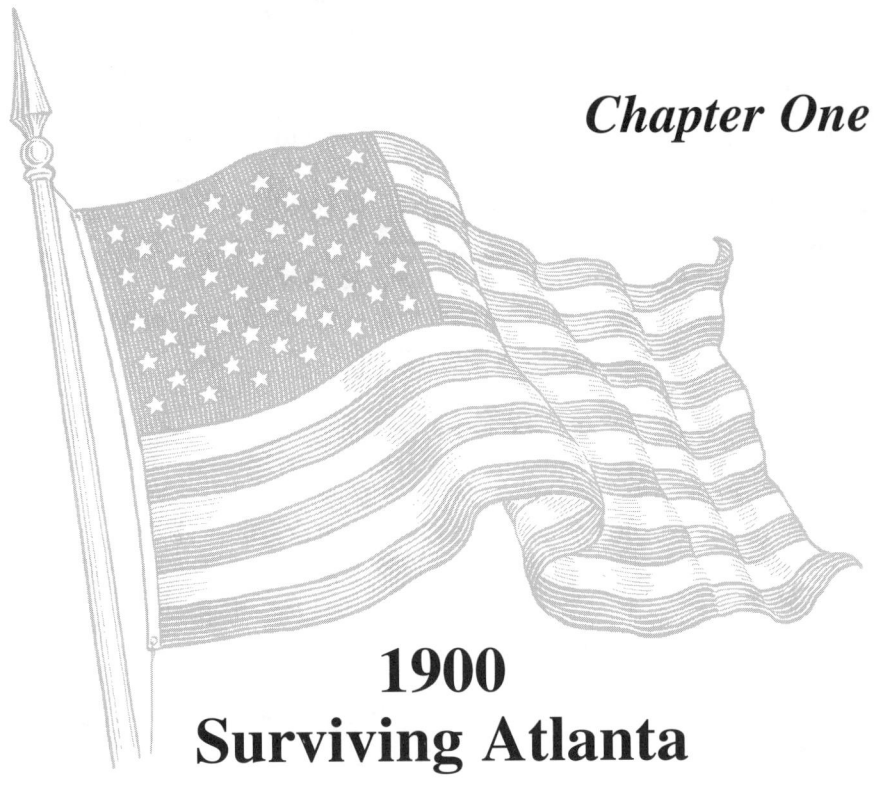

Chapter One

1900
Surviving Atlanta

Herein lie buried many things which if read with patience, may show the strange meaning of being black at the dawning of the twentieth century. . . . For the problem of the twentieth century is the problem of the color line.
— W. E. B. DuBois
The Souls of Black Folk, 1903

*D*ANDELION GREENS *AGAIN*! All we ate were dandelion greens, with the exception of an occasional critter. That opossum we had the previous Sunday felt like it was still crawling around in my stomach. My brothers Bill and Clyde didn't seem to mind, or at least they didn't dare let Momma know. When Salemma got mad, home was no safe place to be. Since Daddy left, we had become the targets of Momma's frustrations. She said she was trying to teach us how to survive in a white man's world, but I wished her lessons were a little less painful.

Born into slavery on a Georgia plantation, Momma said her family was set free by Union Army General William Sherman's soldiers on their bloody "march to the sea." She and the other slaves had taken great pleasure in watching their plantation burn. After her family migrated to Virginia, she had met and married our father, Joseph William Morris. Also born in slavery, Daddy had become a successful leather tanner in Virginia's beautiful Shenandoah Valley.

To please my mother, Daddy had moved us and his business to Atlanta to be closer to her family who had settled there. Daddy drove a soda truck to make ends meet, but Atlanta had killed his spirit, and his affection for my mother died there as well. One rainy Georgia morning, Momma awoke to find a note, and we never saw Daddy again. Her bitterness grew into rage against us, the three reflections of my father who reminded her of Daddy's desertion on a daily basis. Although we knew Momma loved us, we wished we could have gone with Daddy, and often prayed for his return.

A great deal of optimism came with the new century, but things remained the same in the Atlanta slums. My best friend, Jimmy, and I went everywhere together. We spent our days exploring the impoverished neighborhoods of Atlanta's Negro section and our nights gazing at the stars and talking about what we would do when we eventually escaped from there.

Jimmy was the oldest son in a family of nine children. His housekeeper mother had died in childbirth, and his drunken father spent more time in jail than at home. Fortunately for Jimmy, his extended family had filled the void, and his self-educated aunt had introduced him to the world of books. Jimmy and I were the top two students in the local segregated school and often discussed issues ranging from the famous authors to the world events we had learned about by reading. Our teacher, Miss Lilly Johnson, thought our literary interests were unusual for Negro boys, but used us as an example for the other students anyway. Although she was not a college graduate herself, she told us we were college material and provided brochures on Negro colleges, which further stimulated our interests in a higher education.

The stench of the slums stifled the dreams of most young Negroes, but Jimmy and I were excited, having found jobs delivering supplies for a white grocer named Pop Baker who also provided discounted food for our large families and even loaned us books. With the threat of starvation ended, we knew we could concentrate on our bright futures, and we feasted nightly on literary classics.

Our delivery routes took us into some of Atlanta's most exclusive white neighborhoods where we remained in constant fear for our lives if someone took offense to our presence. Jimmy was particularly nervous when delivering to the Widow Oliver's home, as he knew her constant conversation and flirtation could mean big trouble. But Pop would not change his route, at her insistence. One day, the widow cornered Jimmy in her kitchen and told him of her loneliness since the death of her husband, while reminding him that an accusation of rape by a white woman would mean certain death to a black boy such as he. She wanted Jimmy to give her pleasure, and it would be "their little secret."

Although he did not dare tell Pop, Jimmy confided in me that he was terrified, but had no choice. He began intimate relations with the Widow Oliver on his weekly deliveries to her home, and she became increasingly possessive of him and careless with their secret. The widow was fascinated by Jimmy's well-developed young black body and wasted no time in exploring all her fantasies.

One hot summer afternoon, Jimmy lay with the widow after a lustful encounter in her first-floor guest room. The widow had opened a window to ventilate the steamy chamber, and a summer breeze was blowing in the curtains. Suddenly, two white men appeared at the window in full view of the naked pair. Seeing the men, the Widow Oliver screamed, "He raped me," pushing herself away from Jimmy. Knowing death was surely upon him, Jimmy ran out the back door while the men attempted to climb through the window. Jimmy didn't stop running until he was home; he hid in the basement in terror, where I found him a short time later. We both knew he had to leave Atlanta immediately, and I went to find his father who was drunk as usual at the local tavern.

While I searched my house for traveling money, a white lynch mob descended upon the block, searching for Jimmy. The mob went house to house, tearing each one apart, breaking windows, and beating anyone black who tried to stop them. Finally reaching Jimmy's house, it took just minutes for them to find him.

Hearing the commotion up the block, my older brother William and I hastily prepared to battle the mob in Jimmy's defense, but my mother would have no part of it. Tears flowing from all of us, she beat William for grabbing his squirrel rifle to fight them. She screamed that we would all be killed by them and that Jimmy was not our problem. I pleaded that Jimmy was my friend and I had to help him, but she and my younger brother Clyde wrestled me to the floor when I tried to leave.

The mob had beaten Jimmy and his drunken father and had dragged Jimmy to the square to "make an example for the other Niggers." He was strung up, but not lynched, as they had more sinister plans for him. As angry whites rushed to see the spectacle, others poured kerosene on Jimmy and set him afire. The horror of Jimmy's screams, and the white folks' cheers and laughter as he burned alive, struck terror and rage into my heart, which I would never forget. I vowed that someday I would avenge Jimmy. Someday *I* would be the executioner.

A week later, with the memory of Jimmy's murder still fresh in our minds, my family began to break up. Tired of Atlanta segregation and Momma's abuse, my brother William departed for a better life out West and headed for Utah. I began to look for ways out of Georgia by way of a trade school or college education after graduating high school. Anywhere had to be better than here!

Jimmy and I had expanded our interest in books, and each night I had read enough for both of us. I poured over everything I could find, from cover to cover. Another teacher at my school had noticed my literary interest and introduced me to a white man who owned a print shop in Covington, just outside Atlanta. His decision to hire me as an apprentice was a dream come true for me, but did not sit well with his white employees. As time passed, they made their resentment well known.

While in Covington, I attended an Emancipation Day celebration as a pretext for my real mission, scouring the place for local single females. Prominent Negro lawyer Henry Lincoln Johnson, a graduate of the University of Michigan Law School, was the featured speaker. He was a great lawyer who served on the Republican National Committee, and his words of justice and courage touched my heart. I wanted to be a lawyer too!

Back at work, the print shop owner was becoming more impressed with my ability to learn and perform a variety of jobs, and he offered to let me proof copy before setup. But this was the final straw for the white laborers in the shop. When Momma found out that they had threatened my life, she began packing my bags for Baltimore where I would reside with her sister Mary and her husband, the Reverend Ernest Williams. I said goodbye to Atlanta and hello to Baltimore!

A lynching in Mississippi — the horror of the time was prevalent across the South.

Library of Congress

J. B. Morris' graduation portrait from Howard University Law School, Washington, D.C., 1915.
Morris Collection

Chapter Two

1908
Hampton and Howard

I arrived at Hampton in the fall of 1908 feeling as free as
the wild geese I saw flying down Chesapeake Bay. . . .
I was awakened about 4:00 a.m. Christmas morning and
heard a Hampton chorus singing carols. It was the most
beautiful music I had ever heard!

— J. B. Morris, Sr.

*M*Y LIFE IN BALTIMORE proved an extraordinary experience. This was a city with a remarkable number of highly educated and affluent black business people. I found out right away that to do well there, a college education would open the door to unlimited financial and social opportunities and the admiration of many lovely ladies.

My uncle, the right Reverend Williams, pastor of Druid Hill Methodist Church, was a stickler for education and discipline, a belief he painfully convinced me of soon after my arrival. While finishing high school in Baltimore's public schools, I studied every night, worked at the Reverend's church on Saturdays, and sang in the choir on Sundays. Although I had little time or freedom to satisfy my growing appreciation for the ladies, school and the church congregation provided ample opportunities to make new friends and find the comfort I needed.

My experience in Covington had convinced me that I might also want to be a printer and a publisher. Perhaps I would own a newspaper or write books someday. Sharing my ambition, the Reverend Williams had brought me information from a Negro college named Hampton Institute in Hampton, Virginia. The college had excellent printing and academic programs, and I was convinced immediately that it was the place for me.

I arrived at Hampton in the fall of 1908 feeling as free as the wild geese I saw flying down Chesapeake Bay. The handsome uniforms we wore to class made us feel extra special, like the geese, rising above a lifetime of humiliation to a better place. And not only was Hampton full of pretty co-eds, but about 150 American Indians attended as well. What I learned at Hampton would prepare me for whatever life experiences lay ahead.

Founded in 1868 by Union Army General Samuel Chapman Armstrong, Hampton had become a respected institution of industrial education. The Hampton curriculum turned out to be as much hard work as fun. I learned the printing occupation from the ground up and later studied academics. While there, I began to read the controversial editorials of a man named W. E. B. DuBois.

DuBois was one of America's most distinguished educators. While completing graduate work at Harvard University, he wrote his renowned study of the history of the slave trade. In 1897 he began teaching at Atlanta University. While studying the social conditions of blacks in America, his findings led him to write *The Souls of Black Folk*, which helped establish the basis for the creation of the National Association for the Advancement of Colored People (NAACP) in 1909. DuBois also published the NAACP's *Crisis* magazine, and he instantly became my idol. I tried to read everything he wrote, much to the chagrin of some of my instructors who believed in the more traditional philosophies of Booker T. Washington. It was like DuBois and Washington were having an intellectual war for the hearts and minds of black folk. DuBois believed that higher education would lift the black race from oppression immediately; Washington proposed that blacks should be content to attend trade schools, such as his own Tuskegee Institute, and work their way up to equality.

Christmas of 1908 was anything but merry for me. Too impoverished to travel back to my aunt and uncle in Baltimore, I remained in the dormitory at Hampton with a few other poor souls facing a similar fate. Feeling lonely and discouraged, I slept through Christmas evening waiting for the event to end. I was awakened about 4:00 a.m. Christmas morning and heard a Hampton chorus singing carols. It was the most beautiful music I had ever heard!

The reading and spelling work I had done growing up paid huge dividends at Hampton, as I topped my class every semester. Not only did I do well academically, but I also sang and toured with the Hampton Choir, which had saved my Christmas with their songs. About 25 of us performed up and down the East Coast at black and white colleges from Howard University, in Washington, D.C., and Morgan State University at Baltimore, Maryland, to Harvard University, at Cambridge, Massachusetts, and Yale University, at New Haven, Connecticut — and even in New York City's Times Square in the summertime. And the ladies . . . what a thrill!

My wonderful Hampton experience whet my appetite for knowledge, and I applied to Howard University Law School. I had admired the Negro lawyers in Baltimore and thought the law was an occupation where I could use my strong writing, speaking, and reading skills. At Howard, I met the "cream of the crop" of young, ambitious black men like myself who were determined to change America for the better. We represented what DuBois called the "Talented Tenth" of Black America.

One outstanding young man was Isaiah Sloan Blocker, nicknamed "Block" by his friends. Block was a native of Augusta, Georgia, and a graduate of the all-black Morehouse College in Atlanta. We became friends and explored Washington's night life as a team.

Block's mother had survived the bloody massacre at Ebenezer Creek on December 3, 1864, during the Civil War. After the plantation she lived on near Augusta, Georgia, had been burned, Block's mother had joined 500 other newly freed slaves mistakenly following Union Army Brigadier General Jefferson C. Davis' 14th Corps south toward Savannah. Pursued by the Confederate Cavalry of Major General Joe Wheeler, the Union troops built a pontoon bridge to cross the over 100-foot-wide Ebenezer Creek, which flows into the Savannah River, but they removed the pontoon before the ex-slaves could cross.

J. B. Morris (center standing) attended class at Hampton Institute, Virginia, during 1908-1912. *Library of Congress*

Terrified by the approaching Confederates, the group of mostly women and children scattered along the bank. Many drowned attempting to swim the creek, and only a few, including Block's mother, made it across before the Confederates opened fire, killing her entire family. The dying screams of her family and hundreds of black free men, women, and children drowning or being murdered at Ebenezer Creek became nightmares that pushed Block's mother to an early grave. Block burned with anger whenever he told the story, and we shared a vengeance that lurked deep inside our souls.

Not only did I meet talented classmates at Howard, but the social events attracted the most beautiful women I had ever seen. At one such party, I met a beautiful mulatto woman named Georgine Crowe, and we hit it off immediately. Her near-white complexion contrasted strikingly with my dark skin.

Next to Momma, Georgine was the most aggressive woman I had ever met. Her family had come off the Virginia plantation of Lord Silas Crowe, who was actually her great-grandfather by her slave great-grandmother. The "melting pot" of Virginia royalty included her half great-uncle who had prospered in Kentucky bourbon and employed her mixed-race grandfather in his growing business concern.

Georgine had escaped Virginia segregation by moving to Baltimore as a child and living with her aunt, later attending the Maryland Institute of Technology, passing for white, where she majored in textiles. But her love of clothing and thirst for knowledge nearly got her murdered at the racially segregated textile academy. One of her classmates had observed Georgine on her black aunt's porch one Sunday afternoon, and her arrival back at the academy on Monday morning was met by an angry mob. Her white classmates were set to throw Georgine off the second-story balcony to certain death when the academy director saved her life, warning Georgine never to come there again.

As a proud Howard University co-ed in 1909, Georgine possessed cultured mannerisms and expected the same from me. Pleasing her could be a difficult task at times, but her sophistication became a source of great pride for me.

One day, my class was visited by a delegation of white United States

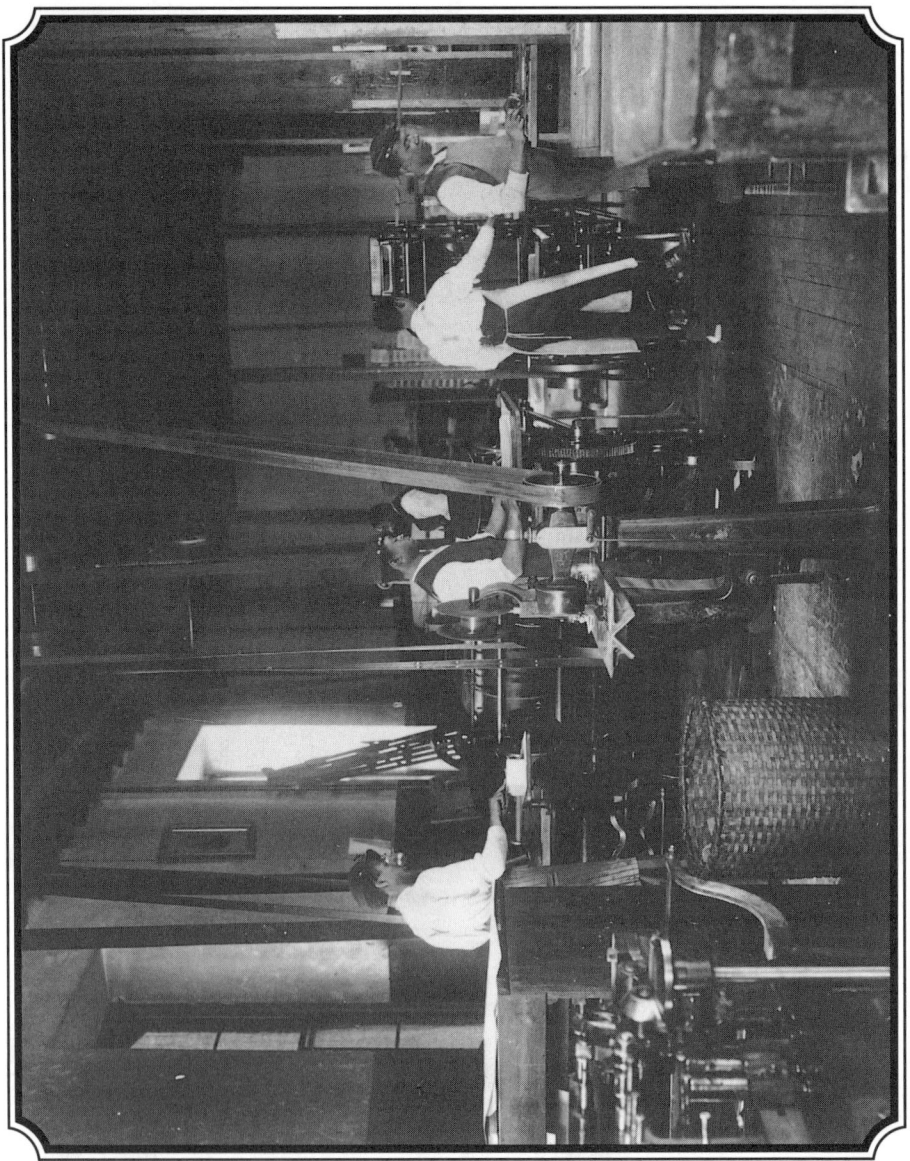

Students in the printing shop at Hampton Institute, Virginia, 1912.
Library of Congress

Typesetting at the Hampton Institute printing program, 1912. *Library of Congress*

Howard
University
Administration
Building,
Washington,
D.C., 1910.
Library of Congress

Howard University Law Library, Washington, D.C., 1910. J. B. Morris attended during 1912-1915. *Library of Congress*

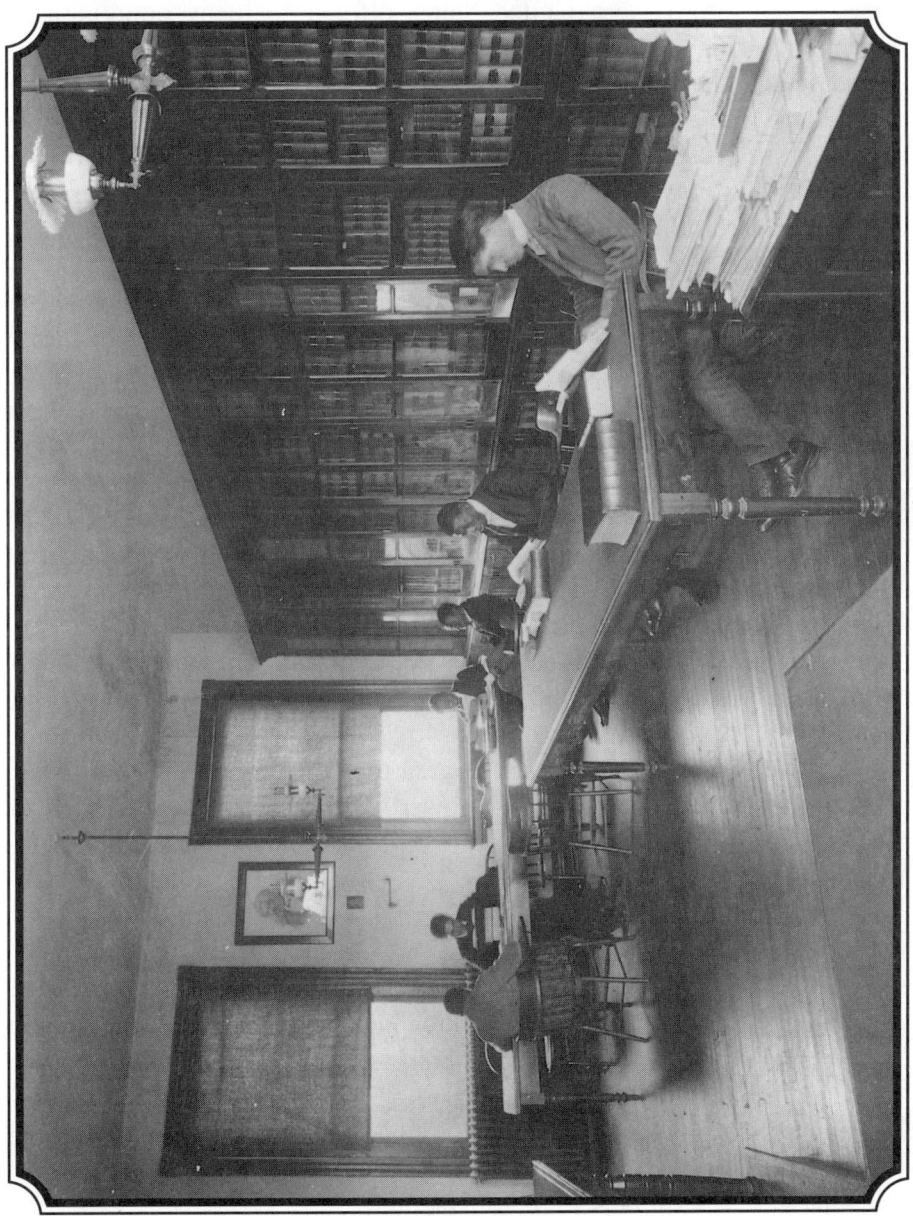

Senators and Congressmen considering federal funding for Howard. They appeared both curious and fascinated by our articulate presentations and seemed to warm to us as the day progressed. Idaho Senator William Borah inquired as to why all the Negro lawyers were congregating on the East Coast when the Western United States offered so many opportunities. Something in his voice lit the fire of adventure in me, and I decided to take his advice and head West after graduation.

I told Georgine I would send for her when I was established, and set out on my great Western adventure. Putting my law degree aside and working as a waiter in railroad dining cars to support myself during my journey, I dreamed of seeing the Pacific Ocean. Unfortunately, instead of heading West, my new job first took me north to Buffalo, New York.

I found Buffalo cold and unfriendly, and worked my way to Chicago where the stench of the stockyards made me nauseous. From there, I wandered to Saint Paul, Minnesota, and took a job on the Canadian Pacific Railroad route to Seattle. I loved Seattle; then I began working the Great Northern Railroad's "Texas Train" route from Dallas to Great Falls, Montana, where I lived for several months.

This rugged but beautiful "Big Sky" country had a history all its own and was still festering in the hatred and fear of the Indian wars. Most of the white folks I encountered were curious about Negroes and fairly friendly, but often made their hatred of the Indians well known to all within earshot. Their prejudice bothered me, as I had become close friends with several Indians while at Hampton and had heard their side of the story. They were a proud people that had been crushed by the United States government and were now paying the devastating price for losing the war. Awakened one night by a powerful electrical storm, it hit me — like one of those lightning bolts — that the Wild West was not the place for me.

The Lakota Indians, or Sioux as the white folks call them, are a proud people who fought valiantly to save their way of life. It was tough to fight rifles and artillery with bows and arrows and spears, but they had made a big impression anyway. Although they had been defeated, starved, and broken, the Indians still terrified the white folks, and I guess in some small way that gave the Indians some satisfaction.

The treatment the Lakotas received in the reservation border towns would rival Jim Crow segregation at its worst. The local authorities constantly reminded them that an Indian life wasn't worth a sack of grain. The Indians often died from alcoholism or at the hands of drunken whites who resided in the dusty border towns that were suffocated by hatred and despair. God help these people to see the evil of their ways!

Realizing I was not far from my beloved older brother, I set out for Salt Lake City, Utah, for a reunion with Bill, whom I had not seen since Atlanta. It promised to be a grand time, and I really needed the rest. After escaping the poverty of the Atlanta slums, Bill had prospered in Utah. He had met and married a wonderful lady named Geneva, who provided an admirable sense of stability to his life. Although they had no children, Bill had succeeded in gaining the respect of his white Mormon neighbors and was known as a shrewd and successful businessman and community leader. It hurt me that he remained bitter toward Momma and had little contact with her, but our love was as strong as ever, and we talked of old times and drank whiskey late into the night.

The beautiful mountain ranges overlooking Salt Lake City and its friendly atmosphere made it hard for me to leave, but a lawyer friend in Iowa had extended an intriguing invitation that my curiosity could not refuse.

Attorney George H. Woodson persuaded J. B. Morris to move to Des Moines in 1916.

Chapter Three

1916
Destination Des Moines

[George Woodson] fought our battles when we were unable to fight. He has done more to make the Iowa negro lawyer respected and feared than all other Negro lawyers combined. His picture should hang on the wall of every Negro home and Negro children should be taught to revere his name and memorize his fine accomplishment.

— Charles P. Howard, Sr., Esq.
The Observer/Iowa Bystander, 1927

*Y*OU KNOW, IT JUST DOESN'T SEEM RIGHT. I went all the way out to Montana and Wyoming after listening to that Senator Borah. A big-time lawyer in the Wild West! What a joke! All I ever did was wait tables and watch the mountains from a dining car window.

I could have cleaned up after white folks back in Baltimore and at least had someone to talk to who could comprehend the English language. Those colored boys from Texas had their own dialect. Well, at least we were treated better than the Indians. Those poor souls were at the bottom of the barrel out there — like being black in Atlanta.

George Woodson, a respected lawyer and politician in Des Moines, promised I'd like living and practicing law there, though all I had ever heard about Iowa was of corn fields and covered wagons. But I thought there was no way the white folks there could be as bad as in Georgia — or even in Montana; those peckerwoods hated the Indians so much that they didn't have enough hate left over for us.

I figured that at least by working a dining car in Iowa I'd get to eat well. Segregation is even worse when your belly is empty. I remember after Daddy left us in Atlanta, we were so poor we would have starved if not for rain water, the dandelion greens, and an occasional opossum or coon that would wander by searching for garbage.

My friend George claimed his law practice was booming, and he was serving as a Federal Deputy Director of Customs. I would have liked to have seen him try that back in Georgia.

I wondered if I would be able get my sweetheart Georgine to come to Des Moines. I knew she loved Baltimore, but if I could stay out of trouble and make some money, she just might come. Hell, yes, she'd come, because I was there — I hoped.

As the train swung around the mountain turns, I wished the engineer would slow down. I had about knocked myself out on the last one. I day-dreamed, and wondered which spiritual I would sing myself to sleep with that night. I was still exhausted from my month-long stay with my brother William in Salt Lake City. Too much bourbon and not enough sleep was tough, even on a young man like me. We had a long way to go before we reached Iowa, and I knew I had better get some rest and be fresh to see my new home the next day.

George Woodson was standing on the platform when my train arrived at the depot and caught me as I stumbled down the steps. His wife, Mary, was preparing a giant feast for my arrival and even had a few of her unmarried girlfriends coming by later. After working a dusty train for a year, some home cooking and pretty women were just what the doctor ordered. I knew I was going to like Iowa after all.

In contrast to the grassy plains of Montana and Wyoming, corn and soybeans dominated Iowa's countryside, and everything appeared to be flat. On the way to George's home, white folks looked us over but appeared to be friendly, and several even greeted George as we passed by. The black community was poor, but nowhere near the blight of Atlanta or the Indian reservations in Montana. I was excited knowing that George and Mary would spare no expense to welcome a fellow Howard Law man to Des Moines.

George had come here with the Army's all-black 25th Infantry in 1903. His unit was to be stationed at Fort Des Moines and had provided quite a surprise for the white folks when they showed up instead of the white cavalry unit the Army had promised. An 1896 graduate of Howard Law School, attorney Woodson's brilliance had shown in a series of impressive court victories; and he had successfully operated offices in Des Moines and in a mostly black coal mining town named Buxton. I thought that if I could do as well as he, Georgine and I could have a wonderful life here.

Upon arriving at George's home, I was impressed by its immaculate appearance and the neighborhood surrounding it. His wife Mary, whom I had never met, greeted me with a kiss at the door like she had known me all of her life. The three attractive young women seated on the sofa looked me over like a pack of wolves anticipating a fresh kill. After a year on the Plains, any attention and affection from these ladies would be well appreciated. Known as a "ladies man" in college, with a "special gift," my love life had died on the Plains, and I was anxious to revive it.

Though all three ladies were beautiful, each was unique, and I would enjoy their company in different ways. Sophie, the first to speak, was tall and slim and spoke with a Georgia drawl. Tracy was healthy but shy. The daughter of a local preacher, her voluptuous shape could turn any man's head. I struggled to keep from staring at her impressive body and exposing my lustful thoughts.

Jane had the prettiest legs I had ever seen. They were perfectly shaped and her rich brown complexion was smooth and unblemished by the harsh Iowa winters. I thought to myself that her lips were as luscious as Georgia peaches.

As I walked all three ladies home that night, I made sure Jane was last, praying for a good-night kiss on those lips. But when we reached her house, her Daddy was waiting on the porch and looked me over as I came down the walk. He asked if I was the lawyer boy from Baltimore, and I said I was. He proceeded to tell me how George Woodson had got him off for murder a few years back. I asked him if he did it, and he exploded with laughter. George, he said, was one hell of a lawyer!

Des Moines' Saint Paul AME Church reminded me of home. The congregation was large and enthusiastic, and many of the women would get overcome and collapse during the sermon like they were Baptists. Singing in the choir one Sunday, I saw Tracy, "filled" with the Spirit, coming down the aisle, gyrating her big body and covered with sweat. Her collision with the offering table sent plates and money flying, and she landed with a thud. It took three of us to lift her and carry her out, and I drove her home in George's car. I helped her up the stairs and into the empty house, and she sent me to the bathroom to fetch her a towel.

I emerged from the bathroom to a slamming front door, and standing in front of it was the nubile parishioner as naked as a jaybird. The next thing I knew, she had pushed me to the floor and landed on top of me with all her weight, pulling at my clothes at the same time. Her generous body was suffocating me. I feared that she would kill me if I didn't satisfy her and felt relieved when she regained her composure, and allowd me to leave.

But not all Iowa women were that aggressive. My experience with Jane was totally different. Under the shadow of her father's suspicion of murder, the local boys lacked the courage to court her. A risk-taker by virtue, I accepted the challenge and worked for Jane's affection at every opportunity.

Jane arrived at the annual church picnic along the river with her mother and two sisters; luckily her father was working and could not attend. Jane and I took a walk along the river bank, out of everyone's sight, and talked about life and family. Somehow, our conversation turned to marriage, and she said she had dreamed about me often, then kissed me with those lips that I so admired.

Before I knew what had happened, our clothes had disappeared. But the pleasures of the moment soon faded at the thought of her father's wrath, and I hastily returned her to the picnic. Fortunately, Jane didn't get pregnant, so George didn't have to defend her father for my murder.

However, after the two recent close encounters with passion, I was determined to be more careful with my lustful ways. When Sophie asked for a date, I hastily declined, as two near misses with death were enough for this young man. But Sophie knew how to turn a man's head, and I was no different. Within a week, Sophie and I were making love every night, until on one passionate encounter she informed me that she was married — and her husband was a boxer serving time in the penitentiary for murdering a man in the ring! If that wasn't bad enough, he was getting out on Saturday for good behavior. My playboy days in Des Moines were over.

Like me, George Woodson was a big reader. His home was full of newspapers, magazines, and books, and I wanted to read them all. I was planning to take the Iowa Bar Exam and find a job that would support me until I could practice law. George's offer to law clerk for him came as a dream come true, and, as a bonus, my social calendar filled up quickly.

Although a young man's virility must be satiated with short-term comfort, my heart remained with my faraway sweetheart, Georgine. The law office occupied my days and the ladies my nights, but my love of printing and journalism went unfulfilled until George introduced me to an impressive fellow named John Lay Thompson. Attorney Thompson was not only a prominent lawyer and businessman but was publisher of a black-oriented newspaper, *The Iowa Bystander*. Founded in Des Moines in 1894 by a group of black businessmen, and originally called *The Iowa State Bystander,* it was the oldest Negro newspaper West of the Mississippi River, and I immediately wanted to be a part of it. However, I found that publisher Thompson had his own way of doing things and was not responsive to my youthful suggestions. I dreamed that someday *The Bystander* would be mine.

Between the law office and my new lady friends, Des Moines had proved to be a surprising place, but my growing ego needed more action. I joined the local NAACP but, as with publisher Thompson, was met with resistance from the elders who also had their own way of doing things.

In response to my love letters and optimistic portrayals of Des Moines, Georgine agreed to join me and arrived before Christmas of 1916. A professional seamstress with East Coast credentials, Georgine quickly found an abundance of work from the wealthiest white folks in town. Though lacking Eastern cultural sophistication, Iowans possessed an "easy-going" disposition that captured her heart.

As for me, I prepared to take the Iowa Bar Exam in June, while following newspaper accounts of the escalating war in Europe. If America entered the war and allowed black men to fight, an interesting incentive could arise. In fact, a lifetime of humiliation by white men could be avenged by this combat opportunity. Even if they were Germans, killing white men and receiving glory for it had a seductive appeal to young black men like me raised in the Jim Crow South — finally a way to release our rage at the trauma of being black in America. And an opportunity to avenge Jimmy and "kick white ass" for the flag!

George was amused by my enthusiasm. His stint in the 25th Infantry had been anything but glamorous. Cleaning latrines, digging trenches, and building barracks for white troops to occupy was back-breaking work for the black soldiers. Not only had glory eluded the 25th, but racial hostility had often threatened its existence.

It wouldn't be like that this time, I assured George. We would kick German ass from France all the way to Berlin!

As I had anticipated, America was entering the war and everyone was excited, especially black folks. Somewhere, lost in our enthusiasm, however, were the specifics about the role Negro troops would play in President Woodrow Wilson's "War To End All Wars."

We all dreamed of parading around in handsome Army uniforms with shiny medals earned for destroying symbols of our lifelong enemies. I was determined to show no mercy when it came my time to be the executioner. No more "yes, boss; no, boss; kiss my butt, boss!" I'd be a bad roughrider and would take no insults from anyone, especially white folks. Besides, George said women love a man in uniform. Hell, I wanted to be more than just a soldier. I wanted to be an officer. A leader of men!

I had read in one of George's Eastern newspapers that the NAACP was pressing President Wilson for a training camp for Negro commissioned officers. If that happened, I was sure to be picked, being a Howard lawyer and a tough customer to boot. I figured I deserved the opportunity to become an officer, just like the white boys.

Early in 1917, the good news arrived. Not only would the Army hold a training camp for black commissioned officers, but it would be located in Des Moines. I couldn't believe it — Negro officers at Fort Des Moines.

I still took and passed the Iowa Bar Exam, but a week later I found myself dressed in my best suit and standing in the enlistment line at Fort Des Moines. Negro college men were signing up all across the country, and over a thousand were expected to start the camp. This was what I had been hoping for — a chance to be an officer and to kick some German butt at the same time. Although Georgine didn't like the thought of my going off to war, she recognized the opportunity and gave me her support and encouragement.

The thought of a thousand young black college men in Des Moines got the entire community excited. Even the white folks seemed pleasantly curious about the arrival of the ebony soldiers. George and I were already boasting that the Howard men would rise to the top of the class. Publisher Thompson, who had opposed the war until he heard about the camp, would write a weekly column on Fort Des Moines activities in *The Bystander*. Even my hero, *Crisis* publisher W. E. B. DuBois, supported the war effort through his controversial "Close Ranks" editorial, urging black Americans to "forget our special grievances and close our ranks" in the fight for democracy.

The eyes of the nation would be focused on the Fort Des Moines training camp. We believed that the camp would mark a time of great progress for Negroes in America, our long-awaited "day in the sun"! Every citizen should come to the aid of his country at its time of need, and I just knew I had to go.

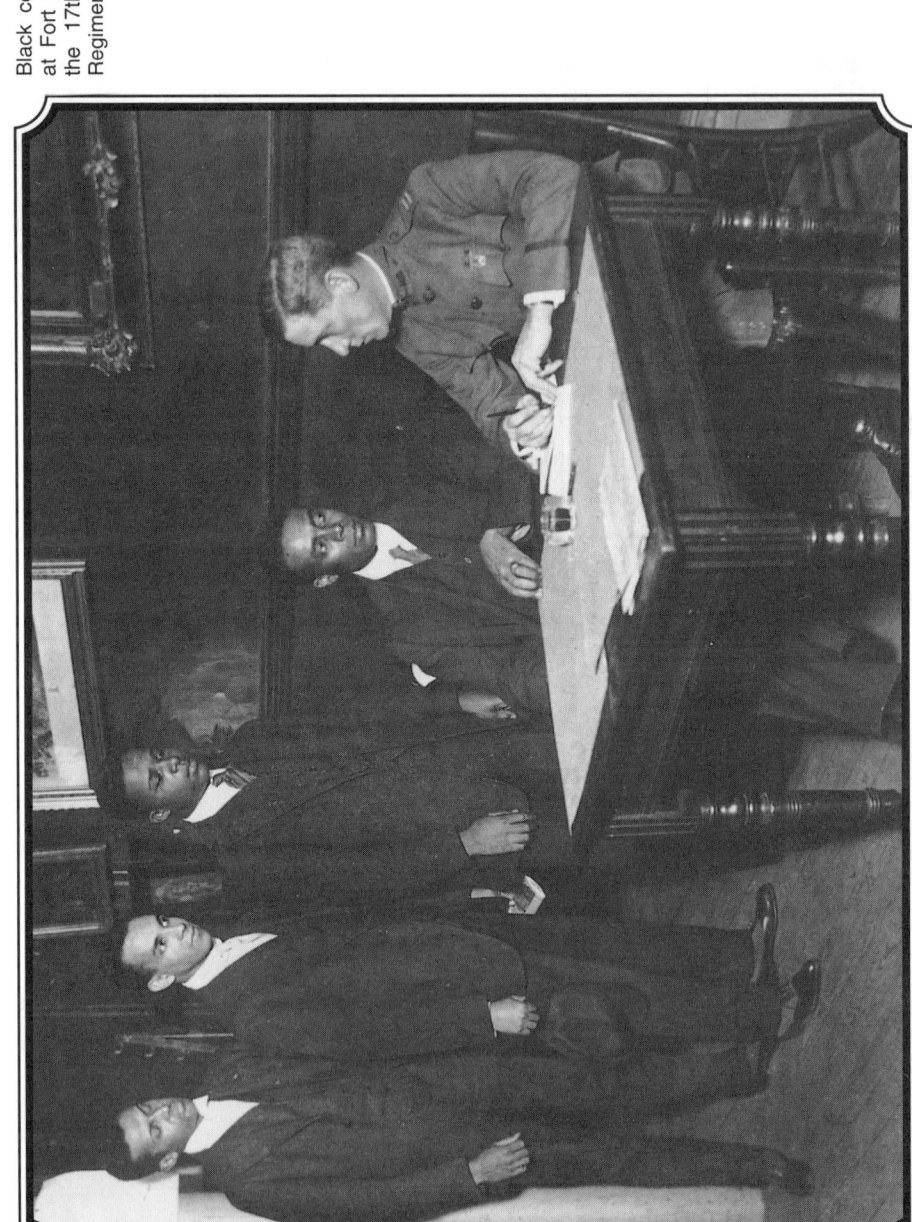

Black college graduates enlist at Fort Des Moines, Iowa, for the 17th Provisional Training Regiment in 1917.
National Archives

Chapter Four

1917
Officers Call

With less than thirty days notice the superb youth, the very best brain, vigor, manhood of the Race gave up comfort, position, future promise and outlook, in their various civil locations and from the North, South, East and West, started on their voluntary march to Fort Des Moines in answer to the call. God grant that their efforts and sacrifices may open a brighter and better day for all down-trodden people of the earth and especially the oppressed Colored people in these United States.

— Attorney George H. Woodson, 1917

HAD FINALLY GOTTEN WHAT I WANTED — the chance to become a "bad ass" U.S. Army officer. Now I could give the orders instead of just taking them. I re-united with Howard Law classmate and best friend Isaiah "Block" Blocker, and we agreed to watch out for each other through this experience.

We were awesome. Over 1,200 Negro officer candidates: 1,000 graduates and faculty, from Howard University and Tuskegee Institute to Harvard and Yale Universities, and 250 non-commissioned officers from the famous 9th and 10th Cavalry "Buffalo Soldiers" and the 24th — and George's beloved 25th — Infantry. We were going to win the war and change the world. We were the "cream of the crop" — the "chosen ones"!

Designated the 17th Provisional Training Regiment, we presented a spectacular sight for Des Moines' 5,000 Negroes and whites alike. Our white Commander, Lieutenant Colonel Charles Clarendon Ballou, former Commander of the 25th Infantry, reassured us that he would declare Martial Law if we were discriminated against in any way. Although his promise reassured us, we nevertheless suspected he was a racist and proceeded cautiously. We had heard that black West Point graduate Colonel Charles Young, whom many of the men knew and respected, was set to lead our Regiment until he was mysteriously retired by the Army for health reasons.

In spite of racial riots at Camp MacArthur, Texas, and East St. Louis, Illinois, where black enlisted troops were stationed, we were rarely hassled by whites at Fort Des Moines or out in the city. We were paid $75 in gold coins and were welcomed by merchants all over town. Unfortunately, after news of the Waco, Texas, race riot reached Des Moines, Colonel Ballou became fearful that the Negro officer experiment would blow up in his face, and he proposed a grand show, which he named the "White Sparrow Patriotic Ceremony," to display the black candidates to the white community.

On 22 July, all 1,250 of us marched into Drake University Stadium and sang Negro spirituals to the curious crowd of 10,000 spectators. We stood at attention in the dusty Iowa heat as a parade of public officials reassured the audience as to what fine fellows we were. After that, we seemed to draw a special affection from the local whites, quite different from the rejection confronting the Alabama enlisted troops across town at Camp Dodge.

Local Negro ministers had petitioned Governor William L. Harding to expel the camp followers who had trailed the Alabama Regiment to Des Moines. Publisher Thompson scolded the ministers in *The Bystander,* much to our amusement, as we thought the prostitutes and gamblers brought excitement to an otherwise boring community.

TO ALL WHOM IT MAY CONCERN:

This is to Certify, That James B. Morris,
a member of Co. No. 3, *of the* 17th *Provisional Training Regiment*
*is hereby Honorably[1] Discharged from his enlistment under Section 54, National
Defense Act, by reason of* to accept commission
He is a resident of Des Moines, *in the State of*
Iowa, *is* 26 4/12 *years of age, and is* 5
feet 5 1/2 *inches in height.*
Physical condition when discharged: "Good"
Typhoid prophylaxis completed July 1, 1917
Served in training camp at Ft. Des Moines, Ia *from* to 1917.
Remarks:

Signature of person discharged: James B. Morris

Given under my hand at Ft. Des Moines, Iowa *this*
day of October, *one thousand nine hundred and seventeen.*

Wm Kelle
Captain of Cavalry
Commanding Company – Troop – Battery.

J. B. Morris' commissioning certificate from the 17th Provisional Training Regiment at Fort Des Moines.
Morris Collection

Captains in Officer Reserve Training at Fort Des Moines, Iowa, 15 October 1917.
State Historical Society of Iowa

All 1,250 black officer candidates, including J. B. Morris, march and sing for 10,000 spectators at the White Sparrow Ceremony at Drake University Stadium, Des Moines, on 22 July 1917.
State Historical Society of Iowa

Officer candidates at Fort Des Moines, 1917.   *State Historical Society of Iowa*

Black soldiers of the 92nd Division ride troop trains to Hoboken, New Jersey, for shipment to France in 1918.
                                                                National Archives

In fact, the college-educated black men with gold coins to spend attracted the attention of many a young lady, both black and white, along with the ire of local males. Numerous white females introduced large numbers of our ranks to interracial relations, pursuing us with a shameless passion. Sometimes, we had to seek refuge in the Camp YMCA just to avoid the wrath of spurned females and their jealous boyfriends.

Those of us in the Lawyers Association had a natural professional attraction to the black physicians seeking commissions with the Medical Corps. Two individuals really caught my attention, and we became great friends.

Dr. Urbane Bass was a native of Georgine's beloved Virginia and a 1906 graduate of Leonard Medical School at Raleigh, North Carolina, who had thrown aside his medical practice to go to war. A brilliant doctor and the father of four children, Dr. Bass was dedicated to serving his country in a time of critical need. He knew our men were going to die in France and told me he would give his life to save them if he had to. I could see the sincerity in his eyes. He was committed to the end.

Dr. John Quill Taylor was a 1911 Meharry Medical College graduate from Memphis, Tennessee. Like Dr. Bass, this man was determined to

The "Always Pal" postcard Georgine Crowe gave to Lieutenant J. B. Morris before his embarkation to France in World War I, dated 5/26/18.   *Morris Collection*

Lieutenant Colonel Charles C. Ballou was Commander of the 17th Provisional Training Regiment at Fort Des Moines in 1917 and the 92nd Division in France in 1918.   *National Archives*

save our lives on the bloody battlefields of France. They would both get their chance.

The curriculum at Fort Des Moines was tough. Both the academic and physical training demanded a maximum effort. In spite of the difficulties, most of the candidates completed the training, and we waited for our commissions. By late September 1917, however, nearly half of the candidates had gone home, suspecting a cruel trick by the War Department. As October began, I was losing my patience as well and feared that my dream was coming to a humiliating end. George was preparing his office to accommodate me as a full partner, and Georgine was planning our wedding when the paperwork finally arrived.

On my birthday, 15 October 1917, along with 638 others, I was commissioned as a Second Lieutenant, and Isaiah Blocker as a First Lieutenant, in the 366th Infantry. Our 92nd Division would again be commanded by Charles C. Ballou, now Brigadier General, whom we heard had been making racist remarks about us, even calling us the "Rapists Division."

After graduation ceremonies, we were dispersed to various enlisted camps for basic training. Block and I landed smack in the middle of the Alabama enlisted regiment at Camp Dodge — and I had thought the Texas Train Negroes were bad! These guys fought over everything from cigarettes to dry socks. They fought each other so much that I wondered how we could ever transform them into a solid fighting unit against the Germans. Half the time, I couldn't understand what they were fighting about or even what they were saying. Maybe this Army thing wasn't for me after all!

On 6 April, Georgine and I were married at Saint Paul AME Church and began planning our future. Our dreams of home and family were overshadowed by the great danger of war in France. We prayed together for my survival.

A short while after I shipped out for France in May of 1918, the Camp Dodge Commander treated the black soldiers to a public lynching of 163rd Depot Brigade Privates Stanley Tramble, Fred Allen, and Robert Johnson for allegedly raping a 17-year-old white girl. We heard later that she was a prostitute brought on the post by her white pimp and actually never had identified the black soldiers as the rapists. On 5 July, a year after we had promoted racial harmony at Drake Stadium, the Camp Dodge Commander cruelly ordered the entire Regiment to stand at attention and watch the bloody event. From what I saw later in France, that incident had a profound effect on those of the Alabama Regiment who had made it to France, branding them as merciless instruments of destruction on an unsuspecting German enemy. For others, this ultimate humiliation crushed their dreams of glory when the Army no longer needed them and sent them back home — a return trip to Alabama segregation.

Those of us shipping out to France spent a long and uncomfortable train ride to Hoboken, New Jersey, playing cards and bouncing around the dusty cattle cars. After arriving in Hoboken, our all-black 92nd Division embarked for France aboard crowded troop ships on 10 June. Block and I knew we were at the doorstep of either glory or death.

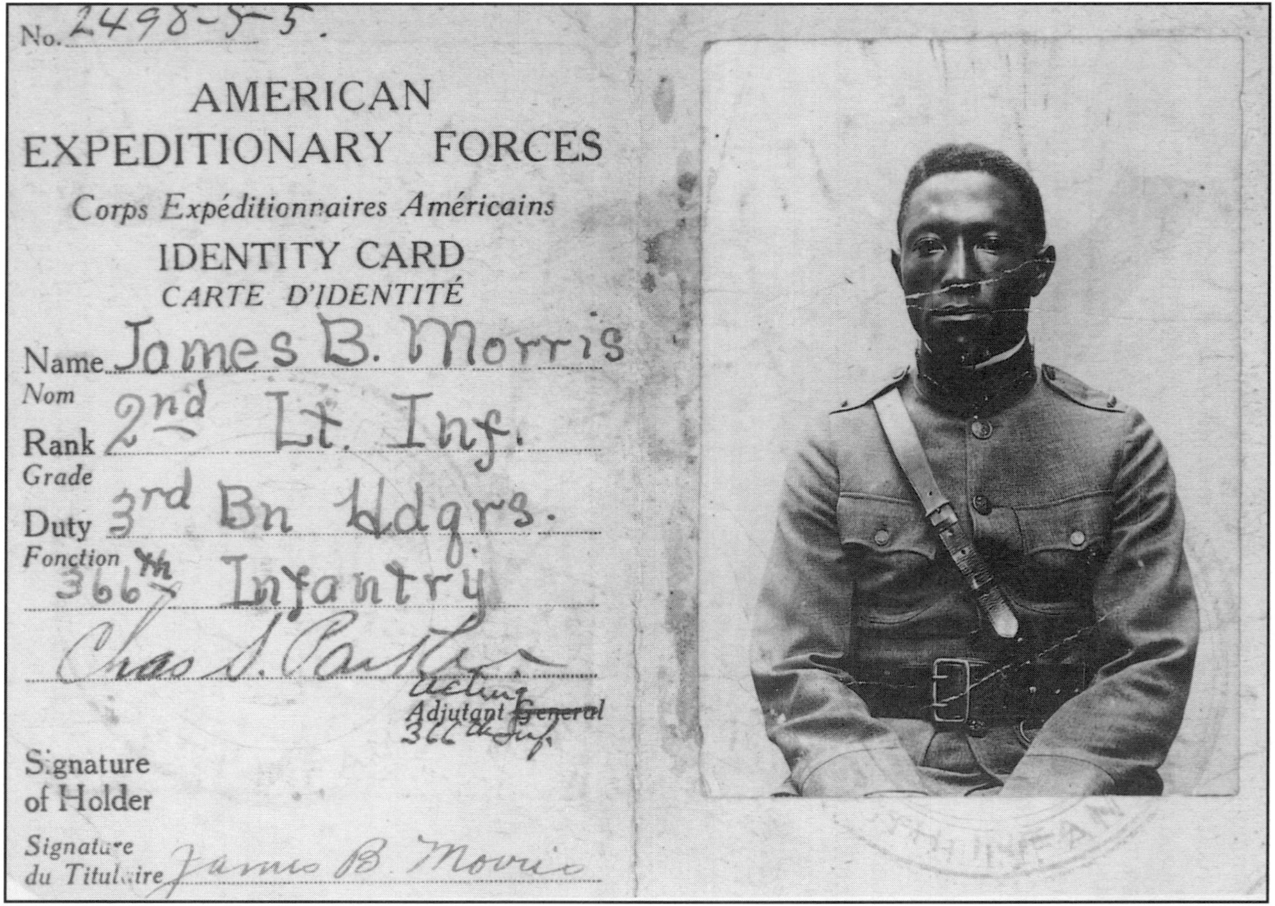

No. 2498-5-5.

AMERICAN
EXPEDITIONARY FORCES
Corps Expéditionnaires Américains
IDENTITY CARD
CARTE D'IDENTITÉ

Name / *Nom*: James B. Morris
Rank / *Grade*: 2nd Lt. Inf.
Duty / *Fonction*: 3rd Bn Hdqrs. 366th Infantry

Chas S. Parker
Acting Adjutant ~~General~~ 366 Inf.

Signature of Holder / *Signature du Titulaire*: James B. Morris

The American Expeditionary Forces Identity Card of Lieutenant J. B. Morris (#2498-5-5), 3rd Battalion, 92nd Division, 366th Infantry, issued in France, 1918.
Morris Collection

Chapter Five

1918
The Great War

Hushed are the battlefields. Ended their marches. Deaf are their ears to the drum-beats of morn. . . . Rise from the sod, ye fair columns and arches; tell their bright deeds to the ages unborn!

> — *Our Dead*, Author Unknown, 1919

*T*HIS WASN'T THE WAY IT was supposed to be. There wasn't much glory in seeing a man with his guts blown out, especially when it was one of your friends. The trenches stank and half the men were sick. At least Block and I would be in the same sector and could cover each other's back.

When we arrived, our Supreme Commander, General John Joseph "Black Jack" Pershing, told us we were going to drive the Germans out of the sector. But instead of attacking, all we had been ordered to do was hold the trenches. I was nearly deaf in one ear from the constant

```
(92)                      HEADQUARTERS
                        FIRST CORPS SCHOOLS
                  AMERICAN EXPEDITIONARY FORCES.

                                        21st September, 1918.

SPECIAL ORDERS, )
               )
   NO.  607.   )              E X T R A C T.

           X              X              X              X

Par. 12.   Pursuant to 1st Ind., G.H.Q., A.E.F. (G-5), 15th Aug. '18,
the following named Officers having completed the prescribed course
of instruction at these Schools are relieved from further duty at
this station and will  proceed to rejoin their proper organizations:

    365th INFANTRY.                         366th INFANTRY

1st Lt. Davis, Irby  D.            1st Lt. Canady, Guy W.
1st Lt. Drye, Frank L.            1st Lt. Clark, William Hoskings
1st Lt. Fairley, John R.          1st Lt. Firse, Dillard J.
1st Lt. Jackson, Landon           1st Lt. Holder, Horatio B,
1st Lt. Rowe, John W.             1st Lt. Thompson, Pierce McN.
2nd Lt. Gleeden, Jesse J.         1st Lt. Wilson, Harry E.
2nd Lt. Lewis, R. Homer           2nd Lt. Brooks, William H. —
2nd Lt. Ousley, Benjamin          2nd Lt. Callahan, Andrew B.—
2nd Lt. Reese, Lightfoot H.
                                   2nd Lt. Elliott, James L.
    367th INFANTRY.                2nd Lt. Howard, Clarence K.
                                   2nd Lt. Morris, James B.—
1st Lt. Clifford, Joshua W.       2nd Lt. Nabord, William D.
1st Lt. Dugger, Edward            2nd Lt. Peyton, James H.
1st Lt. Fisher, Octavius          2nd Lt. Sanders, Joseph B.
1st Lt. Greene, Jesse J.
1st Lt. Johnston, Virginius D.         368th INFANTRY.
1st Lt. Oxley, William W.
1st Lt. Penn, Robert R.           1st Lt. Anderson, Levi
1st Lt. Weare, William H.         1st Lt. Harris, William
2nd Lt. Brown, Oscar              1st Lt. Heslip, Jesse S.
2nd Lt. Conway, Bertram H.        1st Lt. McReynolds, Arnold
2nd Lt. Douglas, Seaborn          1st Lt. Robinson, Peter L.
2nd Lt. Ivey, Louis Jr.          2nd Lt. Fairfax, Norwood C.
2nd Lt. Jenkins, Frank L.         2nd Lt. Grady, William T.
2nd Lt. Miller, Reginald A.       2nd Lt. Henderson, Leroy R.
2nd Lt. Owings, Charles C.        2nd Lt. Reed, Andrew T.
2nd Lt. Williams, Vivian L.       2nd Lt. Richardson, Douglas C.

                        ( OVER )
```

Above and opposite: Special Orders No. 607, of 21 September 1918, listing the new assignments of the men of the AEF. J. B. Morris was attached to the 366th Infantry.

artillery bombardments, ours and theirs, and I had not even been close to killing a German yet.

My life there was that of a typical soldier, but black soldiers were fighting another man's war for the freedom we might never experience. Many

```
(92)

Page 2.     ( S.O.  607 - Par. 12, Cont'd.)

    349th MACHINE GUN BN.              350th MACHINE GUN BN.

2nd Lt. Jones, Charles Alexander      Capt.  Barbour, Charles H.
2nd Lt. Lott, Lonnie W.               1st Lt. Evans, Alexander E.
                                      1st Lt.  Kemp, Frank A. Jr.
                                      1st Lt. Lawless, Oscar C.
    351st MACHINE GUN BN.             1st Lt. Matthews, Dennis McG.

Capt. Thurman, Lesley J.
1st Lt. Williams, Gus                     325th FIELD SIGNAL BN.
2nd Lt. Gaillard, Tacitus
2nd Lt. Hollomand, George C.          2nd Lt. Doss, James Lacey,
2nd Lt. Hunter, Bush A.               2nd Lt. Walker, Richard H.

    The travel directed is necessary in the military service.

        x            x            x            x

            By Order of Colonel Exton:


                A. R.  SUTHERLAND
                Captain, U.S. M.C.
                    Adjutant.
```

of the white American boys were from the South and taunted us at every opportunity, while the French gazed at us with fascination. Encountering white enlisted men was a very awkward scenario for the black officers, as their disrespect could easily mushroom into a fistfight or worse. Usually, they just avoided us, and we ignored them, and the war went on. We had heard reports of our own white artillery units firing on black troops, but I had not experienced it firsthand. If they had done it to us, we would have focused our rage on them, and I don't think they would have liked it, or have lived to tell the story. Be it the Southerners or the Germans, some white boys were going to die at our hands sooner or later. We hadn't gone all that way to miss our chance for revenge against our oppressors.

Sitting around the filthy trenches and singing spirituals through the night to keep awake, the men often told stories of home — boys from Mississippi, Alabama, and other God-forsaken bastions of racial hatred. My stories of Atlanta lynchings paled in comparison to their tales of kerosene baths and mutilations by white mobs.

You could hear the anger and feel the sorrow in their voices as they recalled countless relatives, friends, and even children who had paid the horrible price for challenging Southern racism. Private Joe Smith was a perfect example. Smith was from the Delta region of Mississippi, the son of a sharecropper whose 40 acres and a mule didn't put much food on the table. The oldest son of three brothers and four sisters, his stories of eating critters and dandelion greens brought back memories of my mother, Salemma, and Atlanta. On Saturday nights, Joe's family would host a catfish fry, and the neighbors would bring various dishes and corn liquor to make the party complete.

Joe knew nothing of the world outside Mississippi and would watch the lighted riverboats paddle across the Delta at night. His older and favorite sister, Sadie, would often accompany him, and they would discuss their dreams of better places far away.

Joe said that no black man was safe from a white woman's charge of disrespect or attack and the violent retribution that would follow, and no black woman or girl was safe from abduction and rape by a white man. The sheriff had long ago assured the public that a white man could not be charged with the "murder or rape of a nigger" in his county.

Joe cried as he reminisced about how Sadie had not returned from a trip to the local market and a three-hour search found her raped and murdered in a nearby corn field. Two drunken white men in a truck had been seen abducting her off the street in full view of a crowd of whites, and no one had protested or had even called the sheriff.

When Joe and his father had requested the sheriff's assistance in bringing the men to justice, they were arrested for disturbing the peace and put in jail. That night, a gang of white men, including the accused rapists, descended upon the jail and beat Joe and his father with clubs. After threatening their family, the bloodied victims were released, and Joe's dad died a week later of internal bleeding. Three days later, the two rapists were found beaten to death in the back of their truck. Joe had worn out his welcome in Mississippi.

Joe said he arrived in Kansas shortly after America had entered the war, and he had enlisted at Fort Riley, arriving in France with the 92nd Division in June of 1918. Joe's bitterness toward white folks had festered into an open wound that, he believed, could only be healed with German blood. In the weeks that followed, Private Smith's ferocity provided an example for the rest of us of a soldier who loved to kill.

Block and I cried over Joe's death. A German sniper's bullet had hit him in the throat, nearly decapitating him, as he was relieving himself on a hollow stump. What a pitiful way for a soldier to die, especially one who had survived so much just to get there. When we caught the German sniper, we skinned him like one of Joe's Mississippi catfish and left him for his comrades to find. No wonder the Germans call us *Swartzentodt.* "Black Death" was a compliment to our ferocity, and we wore it well from then on.

After several weeks on the St. Die line, we stopped caring about living or dying and became obsessed with killing the enemy, and sometimes each other. The safety of home seemed so far away while death seemed so close. Killing was the ultimate excess in which we lost all moral restraints and took the hand of Satan himself. I prayed that God would forgive me someday.

I missed Georgine and my other faraway friends, but my current emotional and physical needs were playing games with my mind. I would be glad when we were pulled back for rest, as the looks we had received from the French ladies as we arrived had seemed more than friendly. We talked about them every night, as no one there had ever had sex with a white woman, much less a French one. I wondered what they would smell like.

I had been promised training as a scout in the Intelligence Corps, which would assure me 30 days in the rear. It would be interesting!

After the first few times we fought with the Germans, they seemed to lose their enthusiasm for attacking our position. You could see their surprise when we raised up to stop their charge, like they had seen the face of Lucifer. They left us alone for several days after, and it got downright boring. But that all changed one pitch-dark Saturday night. The Germans hit us with everything they had, including a huge artillery barrage followed by a mass charge. Between the noise of exploding shells and the screams of dying men, I couldn't hear myself think. I was scared and excited, wanting to fight and run away at the same time.

Suddenly the Germans were coming over the top, bayonets fixed and dripping with blood. The white devils I had come to kill were overrunning our trench. I decided within seconds that I would fight to the death, never to relinquish my long-burning vengeance for the murder of my friend Jimmy in Atlanta.

The artillery flashes exposed the white face of my enemy, whose bayonet missed my ribs by an inch. As I gripped his throat, I could feel the life slipping from his lungs, and my hatred made my grip even stronger. Face-to-face, I could see his painful expression as I killed him, with blood gushing from his mouth and ears. As I gazed at his limp body sinking into the mud, I felt my spirit dying as well. He was a soldier, just like me, fighting for his flag. The pictures we later found in his wallet showed he was a husband and father who would never again feel the love of his wife's body or his children's arms, a man whose wants and dreams had died at my hands.

I cried at the bloody sight of my first victim, a life I had violently ended for eternity. The vengeance I had felt for Jimmy's lynching seemed meaningless now. I had killed a man who, under other circumstances, could have been my friend. I prayed for God to help me in this devil's mission.

Then, suddenly, the strangest noise I had ever heard was out in front and coming closer. A German tank was moving through the smoke, and I could not believe my eyes. We had heard about them but had never seen one, and we looked at each other, trying to figure out what to do. We didn't know whether to run or shoot at the ugly vehicle, and it spat machine-gun fire as it got closer, exposing a half-dozen soldiers following behind it.

As frightening as the huge tank was, I realized that it couldn't see where it was going, and it was heading for our latrine trench. Block's men had flanked it to the left and had killed the infantry with their first barrage, as the tank went head first into a month's deposit of crap. The Germans inside jumped out, sinking waist deep in feces, and Block's men killed them before they could even raise their hands to surrender. The sight and smell of their bodies decomposing in the pit made us sick for days.

The bloody stench of the battlefield and rotting bodies often made me hurl my morning rations. Groaning, gut-shot men were executed on site, as neither side wanted prisoners of war. The sheer horror of the place exceeded all my worst expectations. All the murder and inhumanity I had seen in Atlanta was nothing in comparison. I started to believe I would die there, a hopelessness I could not shake.

I was relieved at my orders to report for First Corps Intelligence training at battalion Headquarters. The other Negro officers called for Intelligence training knew Block and I from Fort Des Moines, and we celebrated our survival at a local pub. The French females wasted no time in introducing themselves to us and joining our celebration. It seemed ironic that white women whom we would be lynched for looking at back home were throwing themselves at us over here. They found us a delightful novelty, and we planned to give them plenty of loving to remember us by.

On one occasion, two tall brunettes approached Block and I from across the pub. The one who sat next to me welcomed me to France and told me how she admired our efforts to save her country. A battle raged within me between a devoted married man and a lustful opportunist thousands of miles from home. Regrettably, the latter won out as I sought comfort to heal my murderous guilt. Later that night, I made love to her like there was no tomorrow — and maybe there wasn't.

But her constant staring made me uncomfortable. I couldn't tell if she was entranced by me or was just curious about my black body. Her husband and father had been killed by the Germans, and she begged for my love to soothe her pain. She pleaded with me to marry her and take her to America after the war, and I smiled at the dangers associated with her request, for if, by any chance, I would survive being jailed or lynched for having a white woman, Georgine would definitely end my life for any number of sins. She and the other wives were at home learning French so they could pick up any hint of adultery we mumbled in our sleep!

Many of the black officers were actually planning to stay in France and marry French women after the war rather than return to a racist country. Although American-instigated racism was growing amongst French men, France was still a better place than Alabama or any other Southern hellhole. And deep inside I knew that if it wasn't for Georgine, maybe I might stay, too.

Back at Intelligence Corps Headquarters, we boasted of our French conquests and of the Germans we had killed on the line. I had an eerie feeling that many of the men were giving their last testament, a prelude to death. We already knew that we were headed to the bloody Argonne Forest sector after training, and many of us would die there. In spite of drowning our fears in wine and sex, the war was waiting with the rising sun. We would return to the front, many for the last time.

My murderous guilt was compounded by infidelity to my wife. If I died, would God forgive my sins?

We could see a gas cloud on the horizon . . . a mustard gas attack! It was difficult to put on a gas mask when artillery shells were exploding around you and bullets were whizzing overhead. A stinging pain came from the top of my head. The mustard gas was under my helmet, and it felt as if my scalp was on fire. The last thing I remembered was screaming for a medic.

I awoke in a French field hospital with a bandage wrapped around my head and dried blood in my eyes. Death was all around me, with screaming soldiers in every direction, many of whom were facing amputations.

The stench of blood and rotting flesh made me vomit, and the painful groans kept me from sleeping. In my wildest imagination, I could not have dreamed of such a place — the end of life, the end of glory. Outside were rows of dead bodies awaiting mass burials. It was incredible to me how so many wounded men could be serviced by such a small medical staff.

As soon as I could walk, I received orders to return to the front. The Germans had broken through at Meuse-Argonne and everyone was needed to stop them. I learned that after I had been burned by the gas, a sudden wind shift had blown it back at the Germans. Their frantic screams had been heard all through the night. The white boys said the 368th Infantry had broken and run from the Germans and that we "had better save their black asses" or they would end up in the ocean. As for me, I believed I would die and go to Hell before I would run from those bastards and planned to take as many of them with me as I could.

My new duties as a forward scout proved very dangerous, sending me into the deadly "no man's land" between the armies on a nightly basis. Over the next few weeks, I killed a number of Germans with my knife and with a Winchester Model 1897 trench gun I had taken off a dead white officer. Some of the Germans were exhausted and helpless from the fighting and were easy victims.

I had grown accustomed to killing and even began to enjoy the destruction the trench gun would do at close range. I avenged Jimmy's murder a hundred times, seeking to satisfy my burning hatred for my white oppressors while attempting to rationalize my savagery. Maybe I was no better than Jimmy's lynch mob, feeding on fear and power.

As a forward scout, one of my favorite duties was observation and sniping, and I added German kills to my record almost nightly. One night, a bombed-out French chateau provided a surprise. Thirty Germans drinking wine and socializing so close to the line provided an excellent opportunity to use my skills as an artillery spotter. The first three artillery rounds landed directly on the party, killing them all in a split second. I rejoiced for my victory and cried for their deaths at the same time.

After weeks of bloody fighting, what would become the final battle of the war was to be fought in November near the historic French city of Metz where the Germans had built an armed fortress. Both sides were building up to give their best, and maybe last, efforts. The 92nd would attack on 9 November with the white 56th Division on our left, the French 8th Army on our right, and artillery support from the all-black 167th Field Artillery Brigade. The day before, on the morning of the 8th, the 92nd needed more Intelligence on German troop strength, and we were ordered forward to obtain it.

A bloody stream ran through the middle of no man's land, and we knew German snipers and machine-gun positions were all around. The Germans were running out of men and supplies; the war would not last much longer. I knew that if I could make it through this battle, I would survive. I had already won some medals and would go home a hero. Georgine would be so proud. I would tell her about my affair and beg for her forgiveness — or maybe not. She would kill me for sure!

Something about that little stream made me wary. Loaded with dead bodies and blood-red water, it seemed a formidable obstacle. A perfect kill zone for a German sniper. We would have to cross it to reach our objective. Block and I drew straws to see who would go first, and he won.

I scanned the terrain over the front sight of my gun, searching for a German target as Block leaped across the stream, drawing no enemy fire. As I raised up to follow him, all hell broke loose. Sniper fire came from everywhere, and it felt as if someone hit me in the leg with a baseball bat, sending me head first into the bloody water. I was hit. My shin bone was sticking out of my skin and smoke was rising from the wound. Block pulled me from the water as I screamed in pain. The last thing I remember was looking up at him and seeing blood pouring from his shoulder.

This time, I awoke in a French hospital. Terrified that I was an amputatee, I was relieved to find my shattered leg under the sheet. Block had carried me back to our lines, under fire all the way. I boasted to the nurses

Troops of the 92nd Division are inspected by their Supreme Commander General John "Black Jack" Pershing in France in 1918.

National Archives

Secretary of War Newton Baker inspecting black support troops in 1918. *National Archives*

Graduate offi-
cers of Fort
Des Moines
show the
combat
medals won
with the 92nd
Division in
France, 1918.
National
Archives

A soldier named "Big Nemms," with the 92nd Division, 366th Infantry, clowns for the camera in France in 1918. *National Archives*

that only a Howard Law man could have pulled off such a heroic feat. The 92nd had advanced to within 800 yards of the German fortress at Metz when the Armistice was announced and fighting ceased.

The French doctor told me that I would have to undergo a series of major operations and rehabilitation to restore my leg and that I would be with them for a long time. While suffering through months of painful operations, I received a letter from Georgine. As of 19 February, I had a son . . . James "Braddie," Jr.

I also received word that Block had survived his shoulder wound and had headed for Chicago after discharge. Many of the men in the 366th were not so lucky and had died at Metz. I wrote letters to the families of

those I knew and had plenty of time to cry for them all during my long hospital stay.

My two officer-physician friends from Fort Des Moines were not as lucky as Block. Dr. Bass had been transferred to the all-black 93rd Division under French command as a First Lieutenant and was frantically working on wounded soldiers when he was killed by shrapnel at Montois in October. And Dr. Taylor, a Captain, sickened by toxic gas fumes on the St. Die line, returned stateside gravely ill from his deadly ordeal.

I cried for these men who had given their lives to save us and who would leave two widows and seven children behind to face a harsh world on their own. I prayed for their families and the rest of us riding the fence between Heaven and Hell.

— ★ ★ ★ —

Opposite: Officers of the 92nd Division Intelligence Corps, including J. B. Morris, meet at a French chateau in 1918.   *National Archives*

Members of the 92nd Division march into combat in France in 1918. *National Archives*

25042

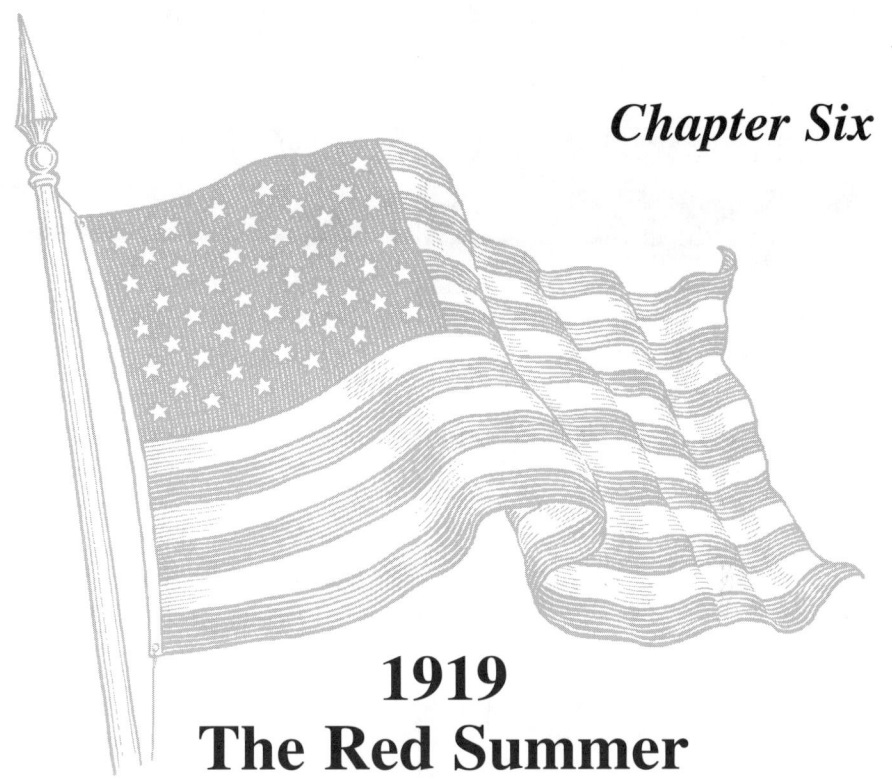

Chapter Six

1919
The Red Summer

The soldiers who fall in the battle
May feel but a moment of pain,
But the women who wait in the homestead
Must dwell with the ghost of the slain.
— *Women Who Wait*, 1917

FTER A LONG AND BORING voyage from France to the States, I stopped at Camp Upton, New York, for yet another operation. My stay there allowed me the opportunity to catch up on my reading, particularly the joyous celebrations for the returning soldiers with parades and tributes nationwide. The reception made my heart sail on the winds of optimism and hope for a future of racial equality and economic opportunity.

When I finally found some black newspapers, my heart sank in disappointment. The returning Negro soldiers in the South had found a cesspool of racial hatred. Black soldiers had been lynched in uniform,

The Iowa Bystander publisher John Lay Thompson in 1920.   *State Historical Society of Iowa*

with medals on their chests, by fearful white mobs all across the South. Up North, black soldiers had been killed by white police and denied employment and housing.

This victorious year of 1919 was the most racially violent year in our country's history. Due to the Negro blood flowing in the streets, North and South, the Negro press had named it "The Red Summer."

I arrived back at Fort Des Moines in July and was reunited with Georgine and saw my new son for the first time. In spite of the horrible racial conditions confronting the returning black soldiers, I was determined to provide a good home and income for my family.

I was pleased to find that George Woodson had taken another partner, Samuel Joe Brown, and that the law practice was flourishing. I was even more relieved to find that he still wanted me to join his firm. Not only did this job provide me with an immediate income, but George introduced me to Republican politics. Des Moines had an impressive group of Negro attorneys after the war including "S. Joe," Samuel Joe Brown, who was the University of Iowa's first black Phi Beta Kappa scholar; James B. Rush and his lawyer wife Gertrude, who were Iowa's first black legal couple; and Charlie Howard, who was a story in himself. Charlie had a short fuse and would come at white folks with fists flying whenever he encountered racial discrimination, be it in the courtroom or on the street. The white lawyers respected and feared Charlie, and fear is a powerful emotion.

Iowa also had a rapidly growing Ku Klux Klan chapter made up of prominent white politicians and businessmen who dominated the affairs of various communities. The soldiers in the KKK were the uneducated poor whites who blamed Negroes for their misfortunes. They made well known their disdain for John Lay Thompson, the outspoken *Iowa Bystander* newspaper publisher, threatening his life on numerous occasions.

My activity in Republican politics landed me a position as Assistant County Treasurer, and I continued to practice law with George and S. Joe on the side. Georgine was making gowns and staging weddings for the wealthiest white folks in town, and our name became known to the white power elite.

Life in Des Moines wasn't so bad for Negroes, although we were segregated. We had our own business and social district on Center Street and maintained a close-knit community with an active YMCA on Crocker Street, and a solid NAACP chapter. But the peace was often disrupted by incidents of racial discrimination in employment, housing, or public accommodations. And occasionally the white police would beat or kill a Negro, or we would beat or kill each other.

As Georgine and I bought a home and raised little Brad, my interest in *The Bystander* continued to grow. Publisher Thompson had grown weary of fighting "the good fight" and was considering selling the newspaper. He was determined not to sell to Negroes who could be intimidated by the Klan or critics within the black community and sought someone with printing experience and common sense. I was the perfect candidate. After what I had been through overseas, he knew I was tough enough to get the job done.

In November of 1922, I purchased *The Bystander* from Thompson for $1,700 and began establishing my production operations. To expand circulation, I would hire additional correspondents and delivery boys in the towns across Iowa that he had missed, where there were pockets of Negroes. Unfortunately, big dreams and small money often don't mix, and my case was no different. Georgine thought I had gone crazy, practicing law all day and working at the paper all night. Little Brad thought I had left home.

After Georgine announced that she was pregnant again, we knew we needed help. Fortunately, my mother Salemma and younger brother Clyde arrived from Atlanta, and our problems were solved. Clyde assisted me with the newspaper while Salemma helped raise little Brad and his new sister, Jean. Unfortunately, two strong-willed women in the house led to plenty of trouble, with me, somehow, always in the middle.

Georgine was not happy with my growing preoccupation with *The Bystander* and the time it took away from my law practice and family. Because few white businesses would advertise in a black newspaper, most of the revenue came from subscriptions. As poor as most black people were at the time, collections were not easy and often took the form of food or services instead of money, which didn't impress my creditors.

At this same time, George had called a meeting in his office to discuss the racially discriminatory membership practices of the American Bar Association. It was bad enough that black lawyers could not office in downtown Des Moines or join a white law firm, but to be spurned by the ABA was the ultimate humiliation. And thus, we determined we would found our own national organization, based on our Polk County Negro Bar, and call it the National Negro Bar Association. The founding lawyers would be George and myself, Samuel Joe Brown, Charlie Howard, and Gertrude Rush, whose lawyer husband, J. B. Rush, had recently died.

George Woodson was the heart and soul of the group — the senior everything. Whenever we feuded or began to lose our focus, George pulled us back in line. His influence was particularly important to Charlie Howard who later wrote that George had done more to make the Iowa Negro lawyer respected and feared than all other Negro lawyers combined. As outspoken as the rest of us were, Charlie was in a class by himself. He had married a Cherokee Indian woman and had the fight of both African and American Indian warriors inside him. He was so aggressive that some Negroes would avoid him, believing that white folks afraid to tangle with him would retaliate against them instead. Charlie's three sons, Charles, Jr., Lonny, and Joe, were a reflection of their father and had inherited his warrior spirit. Our little Brad had battled them to the point of mutual respect, and both families' affection for each other grew.

Although we in the 92nd were America's only Negro combat division and would be in more firefights than the fledgling 93rd Division, the 93rd got the publicity, and Charlie read us every report. He used his strong journalism skills to record the history of the 92nd and made new Eastern contacts that he would use throughout his life.

Although Charlie and I were both fresh out of combat with the stories and the scars to prove it, one look at George Woodson brought us down to

Lieutenant Charles P. Howard, Sr., graduated from Fort Des Moines and served with the 92nd Division, 366th Infantry, in France in 1918. He co-founded the National Negro Bar Association with J. B. Morris in 1925.   *Howard Collection*

earth. George was a real soldier, one who had suffered all we had and more. Amidst hostile Indians and Mexicans and whites, frostbite, starvation, and disease, his 25th Infantry had represented the worst and the best of the American military experience. Sergeant Woodson's drive to persevere under such hostile conditions kept us in awe of this great man. George knew he had our ultimate respect, and he wore the honor with pride and dignity.

Samuel Joe Brown was the scholar and appeals lawyer, Gertrude the community activist. Charlie and I were the hotshot young trial lawyers and journalists — but George, he was the strongest man we had ever known. He was a leader of leaders, and we all loved him for it. He was what we wanted to become.

On 1 August 1925, we gathered in the chambers of Judge Hubert Utterback to incorporate the National Negro Bar Association, and news of the organization quickly spread across the nation via the Negro press. National Negro Bar Association chapters sprang up all across the country as black lawyers responded to the challenge. George became the association's first national president and rapidly gained prominence in the national politic.

Charlie and I kept writing editorials in *The Bystander* denouncing the Ku Klux Klan and their lynching of black men in the North and South. We also criticized the discriminatory laws and treatment being experienced by Negroes across Iowa. Although I had always received hate mail from angry white folks, lately I had noticed white men watching my business. The local Klan were loyal readers of *The Bystander* and made their resentments very clear on numerous occasions.

One Sunday afternoon, I rose from the dinner table to find a dozen white men outside my back porch. After sending brother Clyde to fetch the shotguns, I went out to ask them what they wanted. A short fat man at the front announced that they were representatives of the local Ku Klux Klan and they wanted to buy my newspaper at a fair price. Sporting a nervous smile, he went on to say that "It would be in you and your family's best interests to accept our kind offer." I could hear the safety click off on Clyde's shotgun behind the door, as Georgine and the kids watched the men from the kitchen window.

After angrily telling them to "get the hell out of my yard," Clyde tossed me my shotgun as the white men made a hasty retreat. I added that if they came to my house or bothered my family again, I would kill them all!

After my experiences in France, I felt more than comfortable threatening this bunch of cowards. And after once looking death in the eye, it doesn't scare you so much the next time.

Not only did the Iowa Klan grow to 100,000 members by the mid-1920s, but it ran a Republican candidate for Governor in 1926. Many local business leaders, politicians, and policemen were Klansmen, and they harassed Negroes for pleasure. Fortunately for me and *The Bystander*, not all of the white business leaders were racists.

James "Braddie" Morris at age 12, as a Boy Scout in Des Moines during the Depression, 1931.

Chapter Seven

1930
The Great Depression

I would rather die and go to hell than to let my children know that by my silence, by my acquiesce, I permitted to grow stronger the sentiment that they were not entitled to absolutely every thing that everybody else in the country is entitled to.
— Charles P. Howard, Esq., 1927, *The Bystander*

AS THE GREAT DEPRESSION BEGAN, the Klan applied economic pressure on *The Bystander*, urging my few white advertisers to pull their ads — which they did. Money got so short that I began missing issues; the newspaper was dying. The local daily was edited by a white man named Harvey Ingham. Although I often criticized his *Des Moines Register* newspaper, Ingham and I had become friends through our many civic activities, and I had found him to be a fair man. One day Ingham called me and asked why we were missing issues. I told him what was happening, and he said he would send $100. He also gave me a list of white businessmen

Braddie (sixth from right, top row) played football at Des Moines North High School in 1934, although not all of the team had helmets.

Des Moines Register publisher Harvey Ingham (left) in 1930.   *State Historical Society of Iowa*

for me to call on whom he said "wanted to see *The Bystander* survive." I raised enough money to continue on.

Meanwhile, Little Brad and Jean were growing up, and I took great pleasure in spending time with them at every opportunity. We played baseball in the summer, read books together in the winter, and hunted or fished all year round. Although we had little money, Georgine and I made sure they appreciated reading, writing, and Negro history. Like any boy, Brad had his wild moments, but he became a good student and a good athlete. Just watching my children grow gave me hope for the future and inspired me to be more successful in law and journalism.

Little Brad and I enjoyed pheasant hunting in the fall. The white farmers we would encounter when seeking access to land were some of the nicest people I had ever met. Most of them had never met a Negro and, in addition to allowing us to hunt, would often invite us into their homes for lunch or dinner or even to spend the night. If we killed our limit of pheasants, we would often share our bag with the farmers, and our popularity grew in the rural areas. Pheasant hunting allowed time for Little Brad and I to talk and become closer, with few distractions.

Early in 1933, George Woodson summoned Charlie and me to his home. When Mary answered the door, the look on her face indicated something was wrong. George thought he was dying, and he wanted to talk to us, his "adopted" sons. He told us that we had become fine men and he was proud of us. From meager beginnings, we had become respected lawyers, journalists, and community leaders — Army officers and combat veterans too. His voice faded as he asked us: "Promise to take seconds from no man!"

A week later, our hero and leader, George Woodson, was dead of a stroke, but he had given Charlie and me a theme by which to live our lives. Whenever we would become discouraged, no matter where we were, the thought of our promise to George would lift us from despair.

In Des Moines' black community, everyone was poor — some were just more impoverished than others. Because we were segregated into a few areas by discriminatory housing practices, we became a tightly knit community where everyone watched out for each other and the children. To bolster community pride, I sponsored best-kept lawn and talent contests and held cooking schools for young mothers. Although I felt good about my family and community, my warrior past reminded me of my troubles every night; but a new friend with a similar background helped me cope.

Although we had never met, James Wardlaw Mitchell had graduated Fort Des Moines as a Second Lieutenant, completed basic training at Camp Dodge, and served as a machine gunner with the 92nd Division in France. He was an Atlanta native, an African Methodist Episcopalian preacher's son, and a graduate of Morris Brown University who had returned to settle in Des Moines after the war just like I had. A pharmacist, Jimmy's community drugstore was famous on Center Street, and Georgine and his wife Azalia hit it off as well.

Jimmy and I drank whiskey and talked about the war and race relations late one night in 1935. That next morning, Armistice Day, 11 November, I awoke in a cold sweat. Why had I risked my life to kill so many Germans in France when my real enemy was here all along? I rushed to the office to write a heartfelt editorial about my feelings on the war:

Opposite: Pursuant to his military scholarship, Brad, Jr., attended a Civilian Military Training Corps camp at Fort Riley, Kansas, in 1936. He is seated in top left corner under the tent.

Morris Collection

> *As for the Negro, the war results obtained have been absolutely nil. In fact, more restrictions arose against them immediately after the war than existed before. However, the Negro did profit by the training he received and by new territory into which he migrated which provided new economic and educational advantages. The net results of our participation in the war were many dead and wounded men and a debt we shall be paying for many years to come.*

Times were hard for the Morris family, and our combined incomes still didn't add up to much. Our diet consisted of the pheasants, rabbits, and squirrels that the men would hunt, or fish we would catch, bread Momma would bake, dandelion greens from the yard, and vegetables from the local market. But it didn't seem so bad because everyone around us was as poor as we were. Georgine was often absent, traveling the nation as a branch organizer for her old Baltimore friend, Walter White, with the national NAACP. She narrowly escaped death in Texas and was run out of several cities by the Ku Klux Klan. Her near-white complexion made it easy for her to

Brad Morris, Jr., next to an Army Observation aircraft, while at the Civilian Military Training Corps camp, Fort Riley, Kansas.

travel for the NAACP in the segregated South, but also drew white folks' wrath if she was found out.

Little Brad's 1937 admission to the University of Iowa was a source of great pride. My son was a second generation college man and the grandson of slaves. Georgine and I believed we had produced a young man, athletic, smart, and handsome, who truly would take seconds to no man. Unfortunately, due to my financial struggles with *The Bystander*, his tuition was paid by the U.S. Army — a debt he would have to repay in combat someday.

Georgine founded the NAACP Iowa State Conference of Branches in 1939 and became its first president. She was elected Des Moines Branch president in 1940 and became the leader of NAACP activity in the state. She had been appalled at the racial discrimination facing Brad upon his arrival on the University of Iowa campus in 1937. The dormitories and numerous other on- and off-campus areas excluded Negro students, and Georgine led a statewide NAACP protest of the policies, which I reported in *The Bystander*. She was so outraged by the University's discriminatory practices that when our daughter, Jean, was ready for college, Georgine would personally deliver her to the historically black Fisk University in Nashville, Tennessee.

But in spite of the campus discrimination at the University of Iowa, Brad had a good time while pursuing a degree in political science. He encountered a small, quality group of black females on campus and more on his frequent trips to Chicago. He was having the time of his life, and I advised him to not let his "lust for the ladies" get him in trouble.

Little Brad was by then a man, and, although he was only 100 miles away, we all missed him. The continuing rise of fascism in Europe and Asia would undoubtedly pull America into another World War, and I knew that Brad would not be able to resist the temptation to prove his courage in battle, as I had done before him. I felt guilty that I had created a heroic image of war with my often exaggerated stories of glory, which someday might get my only son killed.

As the Great Depression ground to an end, Brad was soon to begin an adventure that would change his life, and our lives, forever.

Part Two
James Brad, Jr.

— ★ ★ ★ —

The Morris family ties remained strong. When he was in Australia, Braddie inscribed for his parents a copy of his 1941 graduation portrait from the University of Iowa: "To Mom and Dad — The swellest parents in the world. Your Son, Brad. Sydney, Australia, Feb. 1943."

Morris Collection

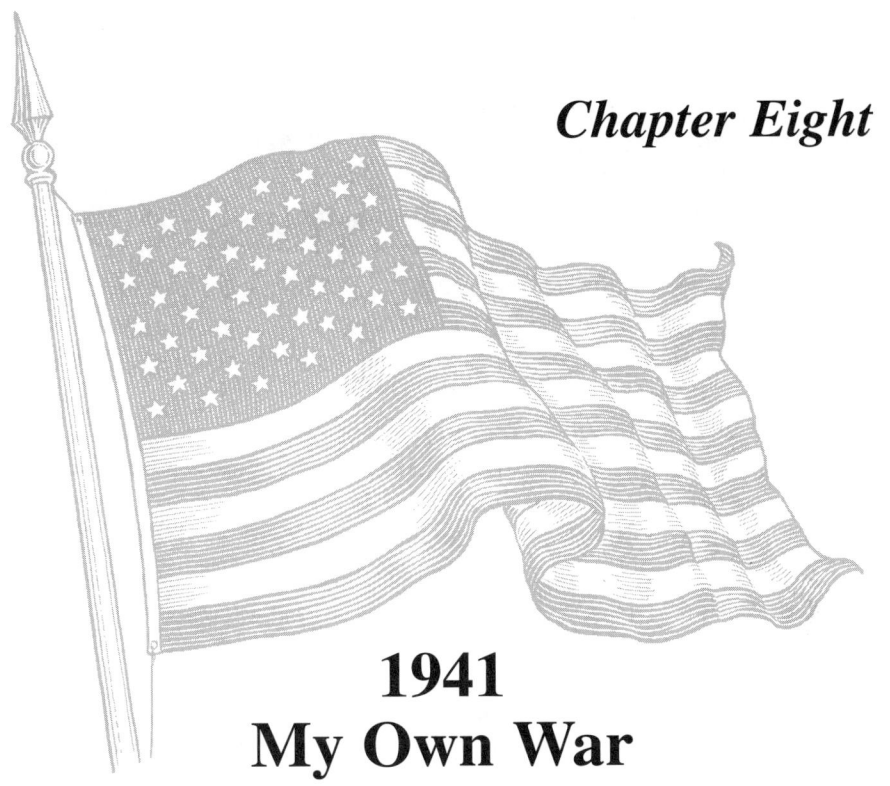

Chapter Eight

1941
My Own War

. . . I believe that the young Negro officer represents the best we have to offer and under proper, sympathetic and capable leadership would have developed and performed equally with any other racial group. Therefore, I feel that those who performed in a superior manner and those who died in the proper performance of their assigned duties are our men of the decade and all honor should be paid to them. They were Americans before all else.

— Lieutenant Colonel Marcus H. Ray,
Commander, 600th Field Artillery Battalion, World War II

COLLEGE HAD BEEN A VACATION from the work-filled environment I had grown up in at home in Des Moines. J. B. and Georgine were experts on delegating authority, and Jean and I were at the bottom of their chain of command. Even Grandmother Salemma and Uncle Clyde got in on the act, and my schedule provided little time to get into any trouble. When not attending classes at North High School, I was setting type or folding *Bystander* newspapers for J. B. late into the night, working on the house or yard, at Saint Paul AME Church, or on summer jobs. Fortunately, J. B. had allowed me to play football, and my female admirers were often more than happy to meet me after practice for some well-needed companionship.

I spent the summer of 1936 at a military camp at Fort Riley, Kansas, in order to qualify for an Army college scholarship program. Although the racially segregated Civilian Military Training Corps class presented its share of obstacles, it further stimulated my fascination with the Army. In spite of the extreme heat and dust, the 50 young black men in the class worked well with the white Commanders and eventually had a great deal of fun. Many of my classmates were from Texas and Oklahoma and had grown up with the Jim Crow segregation J. B. had told of in Atlanta. They were bright and eager, but uneducated and inarticulate, and I chuckled to myself when I compared them to J. B.'s experience on the Texas Train. We explored tanks and airplanes and practiced on the rifle range with live ammunition. We weren't playing Army, we were *living* Army!

My 1937 acceptance to the University of Iowa in Iowa City would provide an interesting adventure as well. After arriving on campus, I met a young black freshman from Chicago named Dick "The Dob" Dobson, and we became friends. Although the housing was racially segregated, we found a fascinating group of black men and women on campus and held regular social events to get acquainted. The black students lived at Mother Ferguson's or Mrs. Lemme's homes and became a cohesive group. We were also only a few short hours from Chicago, and Dob's knowledge of his hometown provided access to hot jazz clubs, good gin, and beautiful women on our many visits.

The Dob was a product of a middle-class family who had escaped the Chicago slums a generation before. His family had migrated to Chicago from Mississippi after the First World War, and his father had found work at the stockyards. After a decade of standing in knee-deep cow blood and pig guts, his father went to work for a local Negro undertaker and eventually bought the business. As Chicago's population grew from countless migrants, Dob's father realized that human blood and guts could be very profitable as well, and the business prospered as funerals became more frequent and expensive.

After growing up around bloody overalls, Dob was never a big meat eater, and the sight or smell of chitterlings would send him out the door every time, providing countless practical-joke opportunities for us at his expense.

I also got involved with several campus activities at the University of Iowa. I joined Kappa Alpha Psi fraternity and enjoyed hanging out with the fellows and pledging new members. One of the fraternity's founders, Elder Watson Diggs, had served at the Army's Fort Des Moines officers camp with J. B. after establishing the organization at Indiana University in 1911.

Although my studies suffered from my immaturity, my social life blossomed in the Iowa sunshine, and I established female admirers all across the Midwest. Following in J. B.'s footsteps, I majored in political science and planned to study law after repaying my scholarship to the Army. The Dob planned to study medicine.

My graduation from the University of Iowa began my commitment to the Army. A large group of Iowa Negroes were stationed at Fort Leonard Wood, Missouri, for basic training, and we reported during the blistering hot summer of 1941. Imperial Japan had won a huge empire in the South Pacific and Adolf Hitler's Germany had established solid footing in Europe as Americans of all colors prepared for the impending war. I had long admired my father's uniform and had been thrilled by his war stories. Now would be my chance for glory, to "kick ass for the flag"!

One of the reasons I am proud to be from Iowa is the record that the Negro soldiers from this state made at Fort Leonard Wood. About 75 of us went down there and almost all became non-commissioned officers. Fort Leonard Wood was my first military challenge, and I performed well, quickly becoming a non-commissioned officer. The black Iowans all prospered, as their superior education distanced them from the poorly educated Southern black recruits at the camp. My background had refined my reading, writing, and speaking skills, and my strong body proved an advantage in the physical training as well.

On Sunday night, 7 December, I had been listening to the news bulletins all day. It looked like the time was really here. I had expected us to be in the war, but not that soon. The Japanese certainly had their nerve in jumping on us. I guessed we would have to go over there and run them into the

PFC Brad Morris, at Basic Training, Fort Leonard Wood, Missouri, 1941.   *Morris Collection*

The chow line at Fort Leonard Wood, Missouri, in 1941.   *Morris Collection*

ocean. There shouldn't be much doubt about singleness of purpose among all the different groups in this country. Everyone would have to get behind this thing if we were going to win and get it over quickly.

The one thing that bothered me was that the Pearl Harbor attack might prevent me from getting home on furlough for the holidays. The consensus among the men was that if we could go home and see our folks, then we would be ready to go anywhere.

The following Saturday morning, some of the boys left for Virginia. We didn't know how soon we would start shipping troops, but I knew that it

Promoted to Sergeant, Brad was transferred to Intelligence Headquarters in Washington, D.C., after the Pearl Harbor attack in late 1941.   *Morris Collection*

After transfer to South Pacific Headquarters in Sydney, Australia, in June 1942, Sergeant Morris, here working on an ammo crate, was admitted to Officer Candidate School at Camp Columbia, Brisbane, in early 1943. *Morris Collection*

wouldn't be very long. When they left, I learned what real friendship meant. Those three months that we had spent together had cultivated some strong bonds of friendship, and some of the boys were crying. The officers even cried. The boys said that they expected never to meet again or, if at all, it would be on the battlefields — or possibly in Heaven.

— ★ ★ ★ —

Soon after promotion to Sergeant, my record was noticed by my superiors and I was transferred to U.S. Army Headquarters in Washington, D.C., as an Intelligence Corps Staff Sergeant. Like my father, I loved the Washington social life and, as a young Negro officer, drew more than my share of attention from the local females.

Unfortunately, my honeymoon in the nation's capital was soon over. In the spring of 1942, I was transferred to U.S. Army South Pacific Intelligence Corps Headquarters in Sydney, Australia. Finally, I was going to war and to glory!

Like J. B.'s sea voyage to France, my troopship was crowded and uncomfortable. However, a stroke of luck changed all that. On my third day at sea, I ventured on deck and found myself surrounded by black men in white aprons. It was an all-Negro galley crew, typical of the racially segregated U.S. Navy. They had never seen a Negro officer before, and they were tickled to meet me. They went out of their way to keep me fat and happy throughout the voyage and surprised me with a duffel bag full of food on my departure, which I ate for days afterward.

Upon my arrival in Australia, I was astounded by the beauty of the country. The Australians were very friendly, even though they were constantly encouraged by the Americans to discriminate against Negro soldiers. I was immediately segregated into isolated quarters and was not allowed to eat or sleep with the white American non-commissioned officers. Humiliated, I began to wonder if fighting the Japanese would be secondary to the racial war for my own existence. I finally found residence at the Inn of Miss Catherine Dupree, a spirited old Australian woman who was quick to denounce the wrongs of her society. Catherine took a liking to me, and I would stay at her Inn on all my visits to Sydney.

J. B. had written that they were training female Army troops at Fort Des Moines, including hundreds of black women for the Women's Army Auxilliary Corps. He wrote that the black enlisted WAACs were turning the town upside-down on Saturday nights, and there were 41 in Officers Candidate School. I wished I was there to see that!

My orders made me a security dispatch runner for South Pacific Headquarters, and I traveled by airplane, boat, and jeep, logging over 5,000 miles per month. Like J. B., I wanted and expected an officer commission and, due to my record and a little luck, my application for Officers Candidate School was aggressively backed by my superiors. During the spring of 1943, I was accepted to OCS at Camp Columbia at Brisbane. My confidence was brimming as I began the school, even though my 700 classmates were mostly white Ivy Leaguers, the "cream of the crop" from America's wealthiest families and most prestigious institutions.

I quickly learned that a fellow had to cut the mustard or he wouldn't

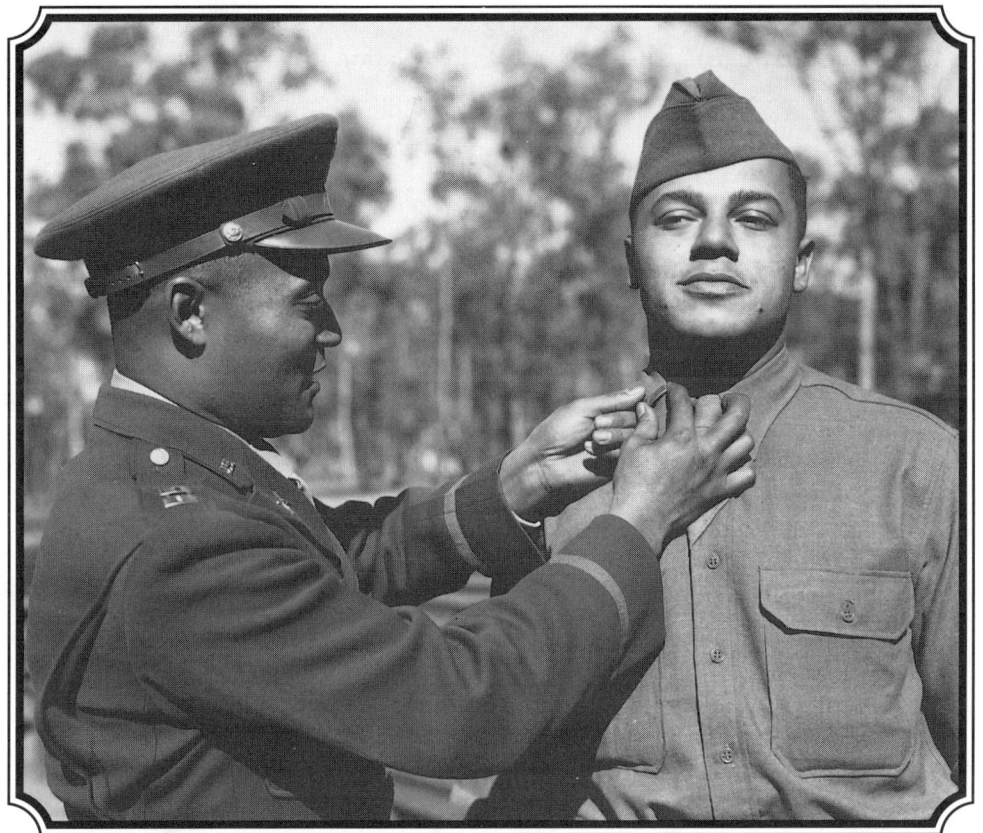

Lieutenant Morris receives his commission from his immediate superior, Captain E. B. Lowe, at Camp Columbia in June 1943. Ranking first in his 700-member class, his story was carried by the National Negro Press. *National Archives*

last. I got up at 5:30 a.m. and was busy until 10:00 or 11:00 p.m. each night. There was plenty of book work as well as physical and technical training.

Although shunned by many of my white classmates, I worked hard at what seemed to come naturally. Intelligence training seemed easy, and I took full advantage of this talent. My immediate superior, Captain E. B. Lowe, had been the first Negro to graduate OCS at Camp Columbia and served as a mentor for me and the seven other black candidates. As many of my white classmates fumed, I received my commission as a Second Lieutenant at the top of my class and was even noticed by national Negro press correspondents Enoc Waters and Vincent Tubbs, who wrote about me in their *Chicago Defender* and other African American newspapers. My story was carried nationwide in the National Negro Press in June 1943.

Lieutenant General Robert Eichelberger addressed our graduation, urging the new officers to "be human enough to hear problems of all men in your command, but firm enough to expend them for victory." Lieutenant General Eichelberger was the hero of the battle for Buna and had been ordered by General Douglas MacArthur to "take Buna or don't come back alive."

My reputation was spreading, and after my June 1943 graduation, I was immediately transferred to the newly formed 6th Army First Corps Intelligence by direct order from Major General Walter Krueger. Known as the "soldiers' soldier," the hot-tempered General Krueger seemed fascinated by my service record and took a personal interest in my development as an officer. His fiery nature somehow elevated him above the forces of racial discrimination within his command.

I drew an assignment to an unusual multi-racial forward scouting unit with the 6th Army "Alamo Force" and was assigned for service against the Japanese in northern New Guinea. The Alamo Force operated as a special task force under the direct command of General Douglas MacArthur and was code-named to avoid any operational control by Australian Generals.

I had my own jeep with a .30-caliber machine gun mounted on the back and a Thompson .45-caliber sub-machine gun for personal jungle combat. My unit included white, Jewish, Indonesian, and Nisei (Japanese American) soldiers who specialized in communicating with the dark-skinned Papuan natives on the island. The all-white officer groups called us "The Smorgasbord," with "WASPs," blacks, Jews, and Japs! But in spite of their bad humor, they would learn to respect our abilities as forward scouts and our integrity as men.

A black man in an integrated combat unit within a racially segregated Army was a strange sight to many of the white troops. They often would stare at me when I passed by. I wasn't sure if they wanted to salute me or shoot me. In base camp, I was often isolated and alone, although some white missionaries would visit me when they passed through the area.

Although the great racial divide often made it difficult to warm up to white officers, there were several who became friends. Lieutenant Joe Cook was a country boy from Nebraska who had never known any black people, much less any hatred for them. Like mine, his father had been an officer in World War I, and he had grown up on glorious war stories. His brother was a B-17 bomber pilot in Europe, and they wrote to each other every week. We planned to go pheasant hunting together after the war, since we lived so close to each other. We imagined that our fathers would hit it off, and laughed over who would win the war stories contest.

One day, while in base camp, we got a visit from John Wayne, one of America's greatest movie stars, who was making a USO tour in the area. "The Duke" had informed our commanding officer that he liked to play poker and would welcome the opportunity to play in our nightly game. That evening, The Duke showed up at our officers mess half intoxicated and with his pockets full of money. He proved to be a better actor than poker player, and after several hours and plenty of whiskey, he had lost all his money. The Duke was not a good loser and launched a drunken profanity-laced tirade against the officers at the table, which included Joe Cook. After using every cuss word he could imagine, he began calling the white officers "black niggers," and that proved too much for them to swallow.

After a half-dozen officers surrounded The Duke, Joe warned him that if he called them one more name, they would beat the hell out of him. Realizing that he wasn't on a movie set, The Duke got the message and calmed down, retreating into the night.

The next day, Joe pulled me aside and told me he had learned something that night. He swore to me that he would fight against prejudice for the rest of his life from New Guinea all the way back to Nebraska.

Unfortunately for Joe, he had little life left. A short time after receiving news of his brother's death over Germany, a Japanese sniper ended his grief with a bullet between the eyes. I wrote to his parents and told them of his bravery and of his love for his brother. Most of all, I told them, he was my friend.

Captain James Brad Morris, Jr., 1944-1945.

Chapter Nine

1943
The South Pacific

I am the only Negro officer in this base headquarters, but that makes no difference to me. . . . This only serves as a challenge to my ability, integrity and initiative.
— Lieutenant James B. Morris, Jr., March 12, 1943

AFTER A NUMBER OF bloody jungle clashes with the entrenched Japanese 18th Army on New Guinea had failed to make progress, the Allied Supreme Commander, General Douglas MacArthur, invoked a "leap-frog" strategy to allow fortified enemy units to "wither on the vine." Our unit, with our sun-baked brown skin, was ideal to lead the Papuan native harassment efforts against the encircled Japanese.

The Japanese were starving. Cut off by sea and air, they were trapped in a jungle Hell in which death by starvation or disease seemed more likely than at the hands of their American and Australian enemies. The Japanese had imposed their will on the Papuan native population after

Lieutenant General Walter Krueger (left), 6th Army Commander, lands in the central Philippines in 1944.

their March 1942 arrival by burning their villages, raping their women, and torturing and killing their men. The natives were natural recruits for Allied Forces and were eager to kill their sworn Japanese enemies. While working with the natives, I had many close encounters with Japanese troops whom we would often ambush just moments after looking them straight in the eye. The starving Japanese were desperate for food and attempted to grow rice in the jungle and on the hills, making easy targets for our bloody initiative.

The smiles on the natives' faces were a sure indication that the Japanese were near and of the pleasure they derived in killing them. A dozen Japanese soldiers-turned-farmers clearing jungle for rice paddies presented an easy ambush opportunity, and they all died without firing a shot. The First Corps' contract with the natives contained one gruesome clause, allowing them to take trophies. After decapitating their victims, they would mount the heads on their spears and carry them back to their villages for show. Unbeknownst to many, the Allies paid the natives by the head, and their bag never disappointed us.

These natives were fond of chewing tobacco and candy. They were hard workers at times. Their pay was very low but they were shrewd and drove a hard bargain. They had very sensitive ears and could hear Japanese bombers coming before we could. Allied troops often watched them and used them as air-raid warnings.

We trudged over mountains that were 5,000 feet high, and it was a grueling task. The natives ran over the hills like deer and almost killed us because we were trying to keep up with them.

Although we harassed and killed the Japanese night and day, they remained, as determined to survive as we were to kill them. In spite of the deadly Allied efforts, the Japanese 18th Army and 14th Area Army would still be there two years later, at war's end. The New Guinea campaign had been a miserable and bloody mission that had cost the Allies dearly. Although we had killed or captured 12,000 Japanese troops on New Guinea, Allied casualties included 3,000 Americans and 6,000 Australians. Disease had claimed 15,000 more Australians, 9,000 Americans, and 5,000 Japanese.

In addition to avoiding being killed by the Japanese, I had escaped malaria, dysentery, dengue fever, scrub typhus, and months of mud, bugs, blazing heat, and jungle rot and was rewarded with a 30-day rest in Sydney before reassignment to the Philippines initiative. A promotion to

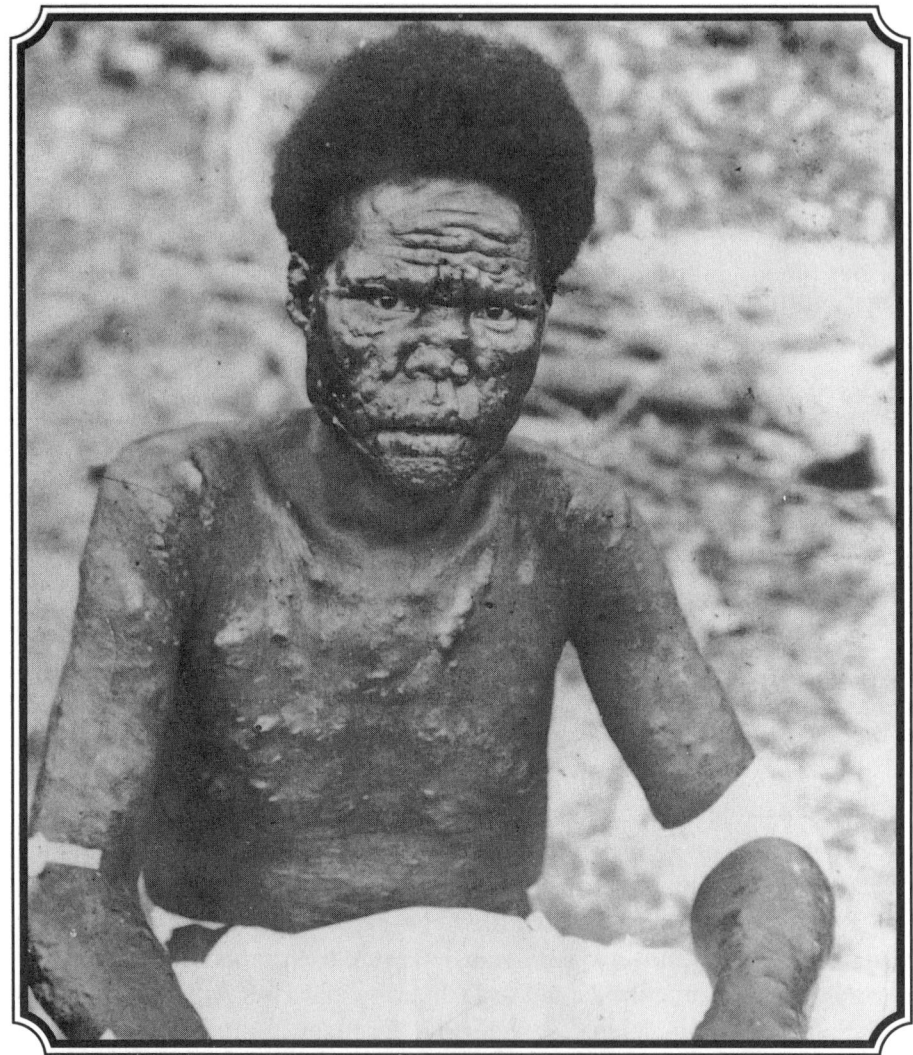

This Papuan native with leprosy faced certain death and was losing his fingers in New Guinea, 1943-1944.   *Morris Collection*

Captain was a sure sign of progress for me, and I regained my strength for the bloody Philippine Campaign ahead. Upon my return, I was disappointed to see the increase in racial segregation facing the black soldiers stationed in Australia in late summer 1944.

In the jungles, if you were wounded, you didn't ask whether the man carrying you to safety was white or black. The segregation in Australia

Papuan Pigmy native Steve poses with his likeness on a New Guinea stamp, 1943-1944.
Morris Collection

Papuan native guides pose for Lieutenant Morris with Japanese rifle, helmet, and sword after a successful ambush in New Guinea, 1943-1944.   *Morris Collection*

was brought on by the Americans. A puzzled Australian said to me, "You are an officer, and you are a black yank?" I said I was, and he replied, "But the white yanks have been telling us there are no colored officers."

Although segregated from most white American social functions in Sydney, my brown skin and promotion to Captain made me a perfect fit with the high-class Filipino population sitting out the war in Australia. At one such social event, I met a beautiful Filipino young lady who seemed as fascinated with me as I was with her. Irene and I explored Sydney's night life and talked of our dreams and faraway places late into the nights. She missed her home and family as much as I did, and we sought comfort in each others' fear of the misery the war would bring. Most of her family either were dead or were Japanese prisoners stranded in a living Hell. She told me she was in love with me, and I hastily returned the compliment,

Captain Morris, 1944-1945.   *Morris Collection*

Captain Morris displays a Tommy-gun in the Philippine jungle, 1944-1945.   *Morris Collection*

Captain Brad Morris poses with Filipino ladies on leave in Sydney, Australia, in 1944-1945.
Morris Collection

Brad Morris poses with innkeeper Catherine Dupree during his leave in Sydney, 1944-1945. *Morris Collection*

although deep inside I knew, that at age 25, I had no idea what love was. In awe of her incredible beauty, I wondered how a war could bring me to such a wonderful Pacific island with such a beautiful woman. I laughed to myself that I had one up on my father's war stories of his French female conquests, and I smiled at what J. B. would say if he could see me now.

I enjoyed the Heaven I was in with Irene before I was forced to visit Hell. This was the light before the storm of the Philippine Campaign.

The orders I received the next morning were for an entirely different mission from the Philippine invasion I had expected. Instead of making maps under Japanese fire, my mission was to return stateside, to one of my favorite places — Detroit. The Japanese "Black Dragon Society" was allegedly operating a recruitment effort for segregated Negro defense workers in Detroit to aid in launching terrorist activities against the United States government.

After spending time in Detroit during college, I knew that "Motor City" Negroes were not interested in facism or the Japanese. However, the paranoia of South Pacific Intelligence Command, along with the short supply of black Intelligence officers, put the finger on me and away I went.

Crossing the Pacific Ocean is much easier and faster on an airplane, and I saw the California coastline in no time at all. A short while later, I was drinking Scotch in a Detroit nightclub in a $100 suit, courtesy of Uncle Sam, with a sexy "Redbone" rubbing my knee.

Stephanie was more than pretty. She was a talented nightclub singer and an Army brat, whose father had served in the 10th Cavalry from the Montana plains to San Juan Hill to the St. Die line as a non-commissioned officer. She had spent her younger years following her Sergeant father from one Army post to another, watching white officers get credit for her father's leadership.

She had made a point to avoid marrying a soldier, and had somehow ended up with a Chicago gangster instead. After tolerating a year of his beatings and infidelity, his gangland slaying had left her scared and insecure. Her success as a singer had made her a local celebrity, provided a nice apartment in uptown Detroit, and launched her into a whole new world. She now desired things and people who could make her happy, and she had chosen me as the one she wanted to be with.

Lieutenant Joe Cook (right) admires Japanese flags and other items captured by Lieutenant Morris' unit in the Philippines in 1944-1945. *Morris Collection*

Captain Morris (lower right) studies a map at an Intelligence Corps briefing prior to the invasion of Leyte in 1944. Note the integrated officer group, with whites, Nisei, and Filipino Commanders. *Morris Collection*

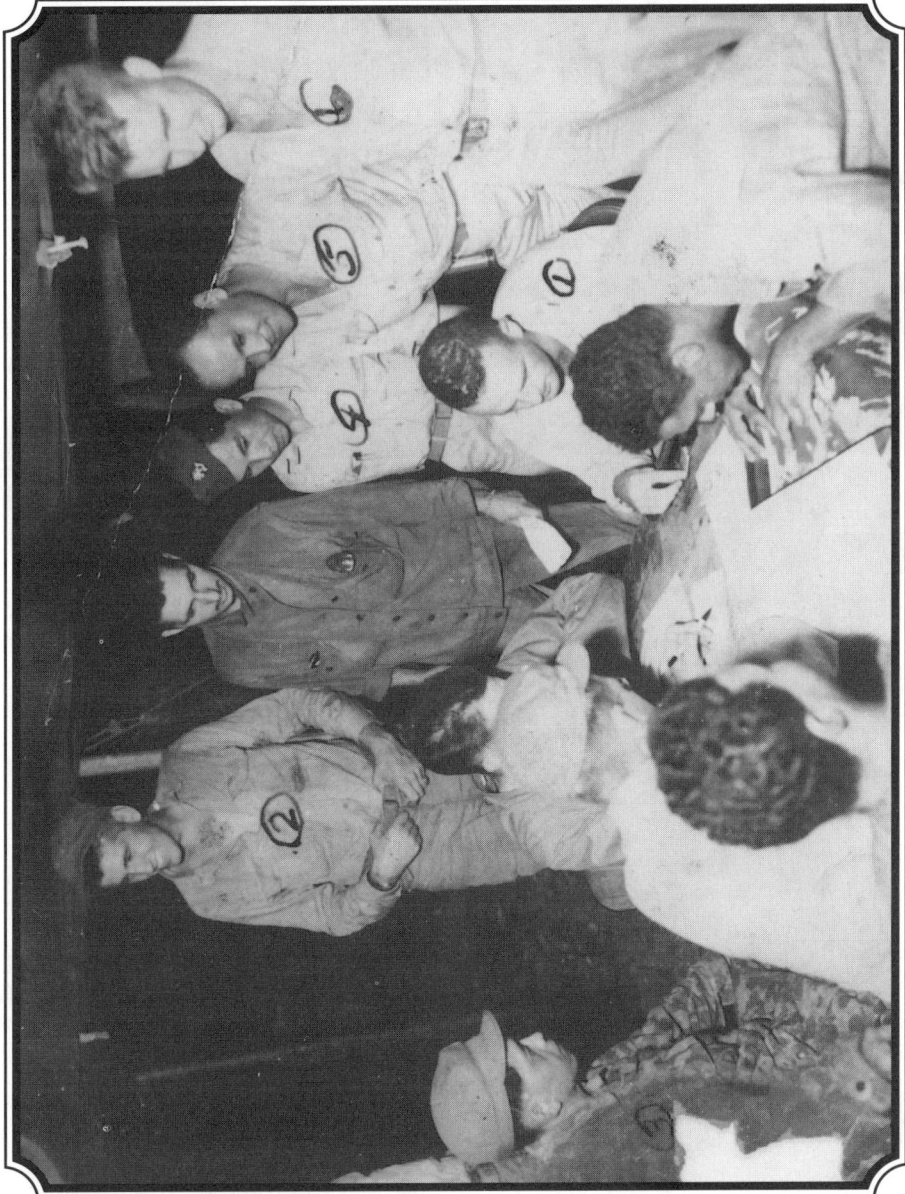

Captain Brad Morris' forward scouting unit loads into "ducks" (DUKW — landing craft) for the invasion at Leyte in 1944. *Morris Collection*

Like a fool, during the heat of passion, I had shared my secret military mission with her, and she seemed relieved that I wasn't a gangster. I had flirted with death on several occasions in New Guinea, and I had searched for a purpose in life before facing the Devil in his own front yard. Fresh from my romance with Irene, and now in deep passion with Stephanie, I realized that I was seeking comfort from these women out of my own selfish fear. I often dreamed about being killed in the Philippines, and knowing someone cared about me would help me face my own mortality.

The big money from the war machine had hit home in Detroit, and almost everyone was either in the Service or working in the defense or automobile industries. Nightclubs and restaurants prospered as money flowed through the town, and segregation didn't seem so bad anymore.

As for me, I interviewed hundreds of Negroes and failed to find one that even knew what the Black Dragon Society was, much less had become a member of it. Most of my targets parted company thinking I was crazy, often providing Stephanie with a big laugh. Although my mission was disappointing, being with Stephanie and listening to her beautiful voice made the long trip worthwhile; and by the time I received orders to return to Australia, I was exhausted and ready to go. After telling her I was leaving, Stephanie confessed that she had married again and that her husband was a tanker in Italy. Relieved, I knew my wild romance with Stephanie was at an end.

Lieutenant Evans shook me awake under the red lights of our ship's quarters. It was "A-day," 20 October 1944, and time to fight. We would be a forward scout unit for the U.S. 6th Army invasion of the central Philippines and would operate within an expected maze of Japanese defense forces at Leyte. Like a dream, both Irene and Stephanie had disappeared, and my next date would be with disease-infested swamps full of 20,000 Japanese soldiers who would try to kill me.

The mission briefing was so intense it fried my brain. The 6th Army was to attack at Dulag and Tacloban and take the airfields at any cost while opening the Panaon Strait for the Navy at the same time. Our success would allow local Allied air operations, prevent Japanese reinforcement attempts, and allow U.S. Navy penetration into San Pedro Bay and San Juanico Strait.

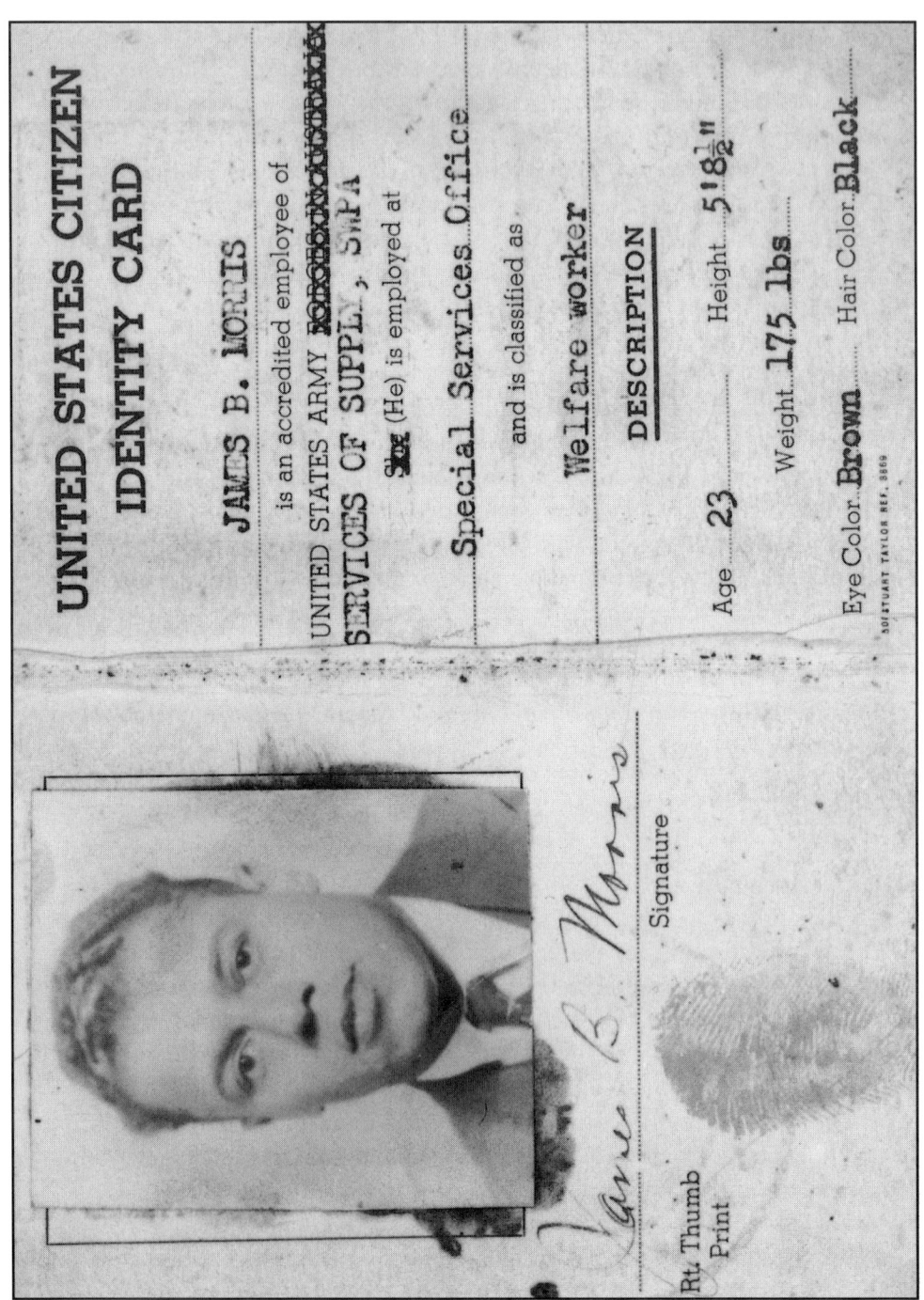

The coconut trees facing the white coral sand of "White Beach" hid several isolated Japanese machine-gun positions that we flanked and destroyed in minutes. Farther inland, the stink of burned flesh and rotting bodies made me nauseous. Piles of dead Japanese soldiers showed the result of their desperation and failure to halt our invasion. A considerable number of Japanese General Sosaku Suzuki's seasoned 35th Army were already dead, and our vicious onslaught was just beginning. My hearing was gone, thanks to the Naval artillery and rocket bombardments during our landing, and my feet were already wet and beginning to rot.

Our first forward scouting mission on Leyte ran us right into a Japanese patrol who fought to the death for a small patch of jungle. But their bolt-action rifles were no match for our Tommy-guns at close range, and we watched their gut-shot Commander die a slow painful death.

Why didn't he run like the others when he saw there was no hope of survival? Why did I kill this man? I recalled my father's story of killing the German in World War I, and, like the German, the baby pictures the Japanese officer carried indicated he was a family man who would never again feel the love of his children. Although I had killed a number of Japanese soldiers in New Guinea, I felt a great sadness for this man, whom I had taken away from his family forever. Would God forgive me for his death? I couldn't find any glory in his murder, though I knew deep inside that it was better him than me.

The Japanese policy of "annihilation at the beachhead" had failed miserably, and they had taken out their frustrations on the native population. We found the Filipinos' hate of their Japanese oppressors to rival that of the Papuan natives on New Guinea, as well as their eagerness for revenge. Not only had the Japanese burned their villages and killed and enslaved their men, but after raping their women had actually shipped many of them north to sex camps for their officers.

Boasting a similar complexion to theirs, I quickly became very popular with the Filipino guides, who were often insulted and humiliated by the white American soldiers. Often when I questioned Filipinos, they would use an expression which means, "You are good." As a man would say it, he would touch the back of his hand and then touch mine to indicate the same color.

Opposite: Brad's ID card for the "special mission" to Detroit, undercover as a "welfare worker," in order to investigate the rumored infiltration, into the black community, of the nefarious Japanese "Black Dragon Society."

Like New Guinea, the only conditions worse than the heat and bugs in the Philippine jungles were the rain and mud. Sometimes it would rain so hard that we couldn't see our hands in front of our faces. We had more casualties from heat stroke and malaria than we did from enemy fire. The roads were dangerous but necessary to move troops, and land mines, snipers, and garrotes were common occurrences.

On 24 October, we experienced an incredible attack by Japanese bombers that shook the ground like an earthquake. They scored a direct hit on our mess tent, frying our cooks like Jap tempura. The attack killed our radio operator and several others, and their machine-gun fire blew my knapsack off a tree where I had hung it to dry out. We were now encountering the tough Japanese 16th Division, which had fought at Bataan, and our casualties were mounting. The Japanese troops were also being reinforced by their 14th Area Army, and we knew we were in for a hell of a fight.

The next morning, we encountered two American officers in a jeep who had been decapitated by a garrote strung across the road the night before. For some reason, their breaker stick atop the jeep to warn them of the trap was missing, and they paid the horrible price. Our forward scouting missions often gave us first pick on Japanese souvenirs from samurai swords to flags and weapons, and we harvested the bounty from our retreating enemies.

We were on patrol one day and reached a native village where we found a lone Japanese soldier who had been left behind by his buddies. The natives told us that there were 20 of them who came back to the village to sleep each night and steal enough food to keep them alive. We set out before dawn so that we could get them before they left the village the next morning. It was a large patrol, and just a few of our men went with us, but we killed them all before they could fire a shot.

In spite of General Suzuki's courageous defense, the Japanese had lost or were losing the ground, air, and naval battles at Leyte, setting the table for 6th Army's invasion of Luzon. Although in retreat, Japanese ambushes and sniper attacks killed many of our men, and being a forward scout often placed me in harm's way; but for God's grace, I would not have survived.

Our 9 January 1945 invasion of Luzon was very bloody, as the 30,000 troops of the Japanese Shobu Group to the north, and the Shimbu and Fuji Groups to the south were angry and ready to fight. I had become accustomed to killing, especially at close range, and would see my victims in my dreams every night. My father's warnings of the horrors of war were true. I had seen death in every way imaginable from disease and starvation to bullets and decapitation. I had already seen enough violence to last a lifetime, and the war was raging on as we contemplated the ultimate invasion of Japan.

I wondered if I would ever see Irene again; I had not received a letter from her for over a month. Maybe she had found another man. I planned to visit Sydney on my way back to find her. Maybe I would marry her and take her back to Iowa. I thought J. B. and Georgine would like her. . . . But who was I kidding? I'd be lucky to make it back myself. Half my original unit was dead, and the Japanese didn't appear to be losing their appetite for combat.

At that time, a very strange thought crossed my mind. I remembered when I first started to college and had a little taste of the scientific theories about evolution of species. I had begun to doubt the existence of the deity, and J. B. decried this shortsightedness on my part. I thought I knew something.

I knew that I was past that stage now. The Japanese had also helped me in this respect, because when bombs are dropping all around you and the ground pitches and tosses like a wild sea, you "believe." It's true that there are no atheists in a foxhole. There are no social barriers or color lines either. Everyone gets in there together and prays to God that the enemy won't drop one in your midst.

Months of combat had worn down my body, but my faith remained as strong as ever and was constantly tested each time I killed the enemy.

One morning I awoke with a burning fever. The medic confirmed my worst fear. I had malaria and would be sent home. Somehow, my disappointment at not being in the field at war's victorious end overshadowed the harsh reality that this disease would almost kill me. Dying of malaria was not my idea of glory. I was told of the 14 August 1945 Japanese surrender while flat on my back, barely conscious, aboard an Army hospital ship headed for the United States. I would never see Irene again.

Sick and thin with malaria, Captain Brad Morris returned home to Des Moines in late 1945.

Morris Collection

Chapter Ten

1946
Home At Last

The passage in your letter mentioned missing me on hunting expeditions and how you often thought of your war and of me while in the field. I am fortunate in having a Dad who pals with me, hunts and fishes with me, and my thoughts are ever of you.

— Captain James Brad Morris, Jr., 1945

*W*E LEANED AGAINST EACH OTHER as the train pulled into the Des Moines depot. Our buddy group of officer malaria patients had traveled home together, trading racial indifference for support in a time of need.

For the first time in two years, Georgine and J. B. had been notified that I was alive, as the whereabouts and health of active-duty Intelligence Corps forward scouts could not be reported stateside. But their excitement at my arrival was dulled by my sickly condition. I had lost 25 pounds, and my eyes were as yellow as bananas. I'm sure I looked

HEADQUARTERS
ARMY GROUND FORCES
OFFICE OF THE COMMANDING GENERAL
WASHINGTON, 25, D. C.

24 January 1946

Captain James B. Morris, Junior
955 West 17th Street
Des Moines, Iowa

Dear Captain Morris:

During the world conflict in which our Nation has been involved, the Army Ground Forces performed its mission with speed and thoroughness. That success was an important factor in the defeat of our enemies and in the preservation of our beloved country.

I want you to know that I appreciate your personal contribution.

As you return to civilian life, you take with you the deepest appreciation of a grateful Nation and a grateful Army.

In the years to come, I am sure you will look back with justifiable pride in the service you rendered your country.

Sincerely,

JACOB L. DEVERS
General, USA
Commanding

Captain Brad Morris in 1944-1945.   *Morris Collection*

like death warmed over. Even worse, Georgine's grief over my uncon-firmed fate had landed her in the hospital on several occasions, and I wor-ried that taking care of me would kill her.

Lieutenant "Little Ben" Johnson, a farm boy from Madison County, Iowa, had gone off to war as strong as a bull and had returned an 80-pound weakling. He was so sick that J. B. had to carry him to our house from the train depot to telephone his parents, who didn't even know he was coming home. During the invasion at Leyte, Little Ben had survived a direct hit on his landing craft that had killed nearly everyone in his unit. He had fought his way through the jungle against incredible odds only, like me, to succumb to malaria on victory's doorstep.

Little Ben's parents cried when they saw him. His father, Big Ben, was the typical Iowa farmer, tough as nails with weatherbeaten skin and concrete hands. Big Ben was a proud man who had fought against the elements and the economy to make his small farm a success. His mother, Jane, was the epitome of a farm wife who had done whatever it took to raise her family and keep the farm, from driving a tractor to slopping the hogs.

After being greeted by J. B., Big Ben confessed that he had never known a Negro and had only heard stories about them. Seeing Little Ben and I, their differences quickly dissolved into a sea of grief. Like J. B., Big Ben had survived heavy combat in World War I and had wrapped his hopes and dreams in his only son. Little Ben had been his pride and joy for many years and would inherit all his father had built. Big Ben spoke of his son's great football game against Creston and his desire to return to Iowa State University to become a veterinarian. They cried and prayed with my parents throughout the night and shared their pain and hope for their son's survival. Big Ben could feel his only son's death in the air. My parents were so touched by their grief that Georgine cried all night by my bedside, begging God to save me and Little Ben. But Little Ben would not survive the week.

To my horror, over the following three weeks, my entire buddy group died. I was the lone survivor, and I held on by a thread. I kept dreaming that I hadn't survived three years of combat to die in my own bed with my mother crying at my side. I dreamed of Irene and of my friends like Joe Cook, and even my enemies who had died at my hands.

My long bedridden recovery allowed me the opportunity to appreciate my own mortality. I caught up on my reading, and J. B. made sure I was well supplied with materials. The news of the racial violence confronting returning Negro soldiers made me sick. Just like the First World War's bloody "Red Summer," black servicemen were being lynched by the Ku Klux Klan in the South and murdered by racist police in the North. What had we fought and died for? What was I going to do about it?

J. B. was practicing law and publishing *The Bystander,* which by then was reaching 12,000 subscribers statewide. In spite of his financial struggles and frequent absence from home, I still idolized him. He was the strongest man I had ever known, and I wanted to be just like him. He had survived a racial war at home and a world war in France, a shattered leg and a trampled spirit, and had prospered anyway — a successful husband, father, businessman, and community leader. I was proud to be his son, and I knew he was proud of me as well.

I arrived in Iowa City in time for the spring 1946 semester at the University of Iowa. I began pursuing a Masters degree in political science and planned to enter law school after that. The campus was full of returning GIs, both black and white. The servicemen had an obvious advantage on the other students, as their maturity and discipline had been solidified through a war. We were serious about our college education, and the faculty knew it. I finished my Masters degree in only one year and entered law school on a roll.

The University was still discriminating against black students in housing, and we raised hell with the administration. I was pleasantly surprised when a group of white veterans joined our protests, and the dormitories were immediately opened to Negroes. When we moved into the Quadrangle dormitory, a group of white veterans stopped by to make sure we were comfortable and had everything we needed. In spite of the racism that persisted in our society, maybe some things were changing. Only time would tell if equality would become a reality in America.

Irene had faded from my memory, and I had fallen for a beautiful co-ed named Arlene Roberts from Moline, Illinois. She was so pretty and smart, I knew Georgine and J. B. would like her.

The Christmas of 1946 was the first time Georgine, little sister Jean, J. B., and I, and the rest of the extended family, were together in good health since before the war. Jean was home from Fisk University, in Nashville, and Georgine from her NAACP travels. I went toe-to-toe with Dad on the war stories, although even my four Bronze Stars couldn't match his proud display of the bullet-wound scar on his leg. We hunted

The Morris family poses outside the family home in 1946. L to r: J. B., Clyde, Salemma, Jean, and Georgine.
Morris Collection

pheasants in the morning like we used to a long time ago and put the insanity of war behind us for a while. It was scary to think that Dad and I had seen so much death and destruction and had come out of it alive.

A proud Morris tradition of military service was born with a commitment to valor that we hoped would never again be tested. Race relations were beginning to change in America and, like good officers, we would take leadership positions in the fledgling Negro rights movement of the 1950s.

A spectacular Christmas snow was falling outside, and Grandmother Morris cried at the dinner table as we held hands and sang "Amazing

Fully recovered from malaria, Captain Brad Morris poses with his mother Georgine (seated, left), sister Jean, and father J. B. in 1946.
Morris Collection

Captain Brad
Morris shows
a captured
Japanese
Nambu pistol
to his mother
Georgine at
home in Des
Moines in
1946.
*Morris
Collection*

Returning to the University of Iowa, Braddie met his future wife, Arlene Roberts, of Moline, Illinois, in 1946.   *Morris Collection*

Grace." The tears flowing down Salemma's solemn face reflected 80 years of hardship from slavery and Virginia Jim Crow segregation to the Atlanta slums and Iowa's bitter cold, a war of survival perhaps more desperate than any of ours.

J. B.'s concentration on carving the pheasant was broken by his memory of the dandelion greens Salemma always had prepared for dinner in Atlanta. Smiling at his mother and warmly touching her hand, he remarked, "You know, those dandelion greens were not so bad after all."

Smiling back, Salemma replied, "Not so bad son, not bad at all."

Afterword

*T*HE MILITARY SERVICE of black Americans has long earned the respect of world observers. Ulysses Lee, in his comprehensive 1966 U.S. Army study, *The Employment of Negro Troops*, quoted an interview from the NAACP's *Crisis* magazine, by a *New York Times* correspondent who had written about a Negro unit from World War I. The unit's Lieutenant explained to the correspondent the regiment's motivation:

> "One of my men came to me several days ago," he said, "and asked me why I had joined the army. He reminded me that I was above draft age and he wanted me to tell him what I was fighting for. I told him I was fighting for what the flag meant to the Negroes in the United States. I told him I was fighting because I wanted other oppressed people to know the meaning of democracy and enjoy it. I told him that millions of Americans fought for us Negroes to get it and now it

was only right that we should fight for all we were worth to help
other people get the same thing. . . .

"I told him that now is our opportunity to prove what we can
do. . . ."

— "The Looking Glass: Over There," *The Crisis,*
XVI (August 1918)

The Crisis, in September 1918, also quoted a United Press report stat-
ing that

American Negro troops proved their value as fighters in the
line east of Verdun. . . . The Germans attempted a raid in that
sector but were completely repulsed by the Negroes. . . .

In the midst of this inferno the Negroes coolly stuck to their
posts, . . . keeping up such a steady barrage that the German
infantry failed to penetrate the American lines. The Americans
miraculously sustained only two wounded.

— *The Crisis*, XVI (September 1918)

Yet, while the "skill and courage of Negro soldiers," as Dr. Lee stated,
were widely reported, "beneath the surface other rumors were running
thick and fast" — charges of cowardice mixed with reports of Negro
troops abused by white officers; systematic attempts to "break" and
demote Negro officers; assignment to "the most dangerous battle zones
and as labor troops where the work was the hardest". . . and more. And in
summation, it was realized that there was an overriding failure of military
"organization," "morale," and thus "accomplishment."

Ulysses Lee added, ". . . The picture of Negro participation in World
War I became a clouded one."

By 1945, toward the end of World War II, General Douglas MacArthur
boldly declared, ". . . Race and color have nothing whatever to do with
fighting ability. . . ."

And at about the same time, Lieutenant Colonel Marcus H. Ray, Commander, 600th Field Artillery Battalion, concluded:

. . . I believe that the young Negro officer represents the best we
have to offer. . . . Those who performed in a superior manner
and those who died in the proper performance of their assigned

duties are our men of the decade and all honor should be paid
to them. They were Americans before all else.
> — *in* Ulysses Lee, *The Employment of Negro Troops*, 589

Military men of black American families, like J. B. Morris and his son,
James Brad, have proved their honor . . . and have sustained their tradition.

Sources

Chicago Defender, Enoch Waters, June 1943.

Des Moines Register & Tribune, June 10, 1971.

DuBois, W.E.B. *The Souls of Black Folk: Essays and Sketches.* Chicago: A. C. McClurg, 1903.

DuBois, W.E.B., "The Reward," *The Crisis*, XVI (September 1918).

Early, Gerald, ed. *"Ain't But a Place: An Anthology of African American Writings about St. Louis.* St. Louis: Missouri Historical Society Press, 1998.

Lee, Ulysses. *The Employment of Negro Troops. United States Army in World War II Special Studies.* Washington, D.C.: Office of the Chief of Military History, United States Army, 1966.

National Negro, Press Release, Vincent Tubbs, June 1943.

Our Dead. Author Unknown. 1919.

The Iowa Bystander, J. B. Morris editorials, November 15, 1935, June 10, 1971.

The Observer/The Iowa Bystander, 1927.

Women Who Wait, in *History and Views of Colored Offiers Training Camps*, John L. Thompson. Des Moines, IA: *The Bystander* Publishing Co., 1917.

Appendix — From the Morris Album

★ ★ ★

Sister Jean and brother Braddie Morris at Salt Air on the Great Salt Lake, 1927.
Morris Collection

Below: Braddie, in Des Moines in 1936, showing his athletic build that proved to be an asset during his military career.
Morris Collection

Author Robert (left) and brothers Braddie, Jr. (right) and William (center), 1963.

Morris Collection

A pretty girl and a car made Braddie's time pass quickly at the University of Iowa, 1938.
Morris Collection

Below: Braddie (right) and "The Dob" always found the ladies on the lake in Chicago, 1938.
Morris Collection

Braddie (second from right, lower row) poses with members of Kappa Alpha Psi fraternity, Gamma Chapter, at the University of Iowa in 1938.   *Morris Collection*

Clowning with "The Dob" on the University of Iowa campus in November 1938. *Morris Collection*

Left and below: More clowning with "The Dob" on the University of Iowa campus in November 1937.
Morris Collection

Arlene Roberts (right) on the University of Iowa campus, 1946.
Morris Collection

Braddie (right) in front of 942 Iowa Avenue in Iowa City in 1938. The home was an Underground Railroad stop during the Civil War.
Morris Collection

L to r: J. B., Salemma with Brad III, and Brad, Jr., 1950.   *Morris Collection*

The author's daughter Jessica (12), sons Robert, Jr. (9) and Brandon (6).

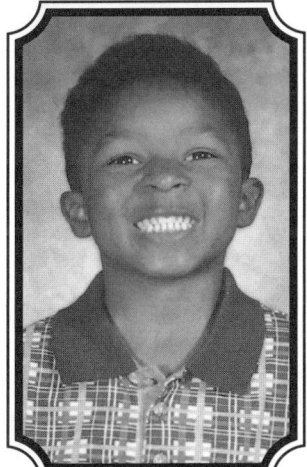

The author's nephew William Stephen Morris, Jr. (6).

The author's wife Vivian Vaughn-Morris with firstborn Jessica 1988.

Index

by Lori L. Daniel